D0343595

TRAIN YOUR BRAIN

TRAIN YOUR BRAIN

The ultimate 21 day mental skills programme for peak performance

DR HARRY ALDER

PIATKUS

To Mrs Daisy Alder,
her only boy's most dependable fan

First published in hardback in 1997 by
Judy Piatkus (Publishers) Ltd
5 Windmill Street, London W1P 1HF

First paperback edition published in 1998

**The moral right of the author
has been asserted**

*A catalogue record for this book is
available from the British Library*

ISBN 0-7499-1809-8

Designed by Chris Warner
Data capture and manipulation by
Professional Data Bureau, London SW17
Printed and bound in Great Britain by
Mackays of Chatham PLC

Contents

INTRODUCTION

A business colleague had an important report to write affecting his company's future. Although he had several weeks to think about it, he was at a loss as to how to approach the task and not a little anxious as the deadline drew nearer. At about 3 o'clock one Saturday morning he awoke with his mind buzzing with ideas about how the report could be tackled. He got out of bed and started writing. By late morning he had completely written the report, which included recommendations and insights that surprised even him. With hardly a correction the report was presented, accepted and proved of real benefit to the company, possibly ensuring its very survival. He described that as 'peak performance', although he could not begin to explain what had happened and did not know how he might re-create such a productive, enjoyable experience.

That's a common enough story, but where did these ideas come from? Why did they not occur to him in the normal course of work when he was consciously thinking about the issues? Why did it happen in the middle of the night? And why was the whole experience so pleasurable, as well as effective and timely? In this book you will find the answers to these and other questions that will enable you to operate at your best and achieve many of your unfulfilled goals and ambitions. You will be able to train your brain to think more creatively and act more confidently. The result will be peak performance.

What makes my colleague's kind of experience appealing is

that it doesn't depend on the pain, perspiration and persistence often associated with great achievement. It seems to defy all the text book injunctions of planning and logical thinking. Imagination rather than will power seems to be at work here. Time stands still. Concentration is easy. Productivity is way up. It is more associated with the fun and fascination of childlike learning and discovery, the natural way to personal growth and achievement. Somehow experiences like this, which can border on the mystical, account for high performance and achievement in every walk of life. Understood and harnessed, they are the secret of top performance. There is no magic, other than the magic of your fantastic brain. You just need the information and know-how to train your brain.

For a start, there is now the information available to help you understand how to use your *mind* better to achieve more — much more. Developments in neurophysiology, helped by the latest technology in real-time brain scanning, and whole new branches of knowledge such as neuro-linguistic programming (NLP), are making this possible. So the information age, where we must rely on our minds rather than our muscles, can now benefit you in a special and very personal way.

You probably feel you are capable of achieving more. You may have goals and ambitions so far unfulfilled. Or you may be open to the possibility of extending your horizons, but lack confidence and self-belief and the knowledge of what to do. This book will show you just what you can aspire to, and how to achieve those aspirations. Training your brain to peak performance can become a personal possibility and in turn a reality.

It starts in the mind. But this is not just *positive* thinking. It is *better* thinking; a special kind of thinking that uses your innate creative, intuitive, sometimes unconscious powers. Just a few aspects of this new knowledge can give you a level of control over your thinking, behaviour and achievement that would have been incredible just a few years ago. This book brings together this vital knowledge into an accessible, practical format that you can immediately benefit from. It gives an ordinary person the information he or she needs to achieve extraordinary things.

You can enjoy peak performance in any area you choose. There are a few principles to understand and some simple techniques to learn. But the secret of achieving your best boils down to understanding, at least in part, and trusting, rather more fully, the remarkable mental powers you already have.

1

FLASHES AND FLOW

'EUREKA!' AND 'BEING IN THE ZONE'

There are two important aspects of peak performance that together account for just about the whole phenomenon of excellence, mastery, human achievement and any terms we care to use. One is best described as the 'Eureka!' you probably first learnt of in the context of Archimedes who jumped out of his bath having had a flash of inspiration that solved an important scientific problem. But it is the same sort of brainwave or flash of inspiration that we all experience from time to time. Most people will recognise some or all of the following.

➤ Suddenly, when least expecting it, remembering the name of a person you have earlier been racking your brain over.

➤ Getting in a flash — maybe in the shower, during the night or when out walking — the solution to something that has been troubling you, as if from outside yourself.

➤ Spotting a new, original angle on a problem that pleasantly surprises you, and unblocks an impasse.

➤ Dreaming up some creative breakthrough, the plot of a novel, a new product, a great corporate strategy — something well beyond your day-to-day thinking level.

➤ Having an insight, perhaps into a personal situation, that seems almost extrasensory — maybe a so-called first impression — and which turns out to be accurate.

➤ Suddenly knowing with confidence which decision you have to take, whether at work or personally, say about a job, house or person you should choose, or even which golf club to pick.

Eureka experiences come in many varieties and to different degrees, of course. How many times have you been able to remember something by thinking or doing something completely different, rather than trying to force it, for example? Or received a flash of insight or answers to pressing problems during the night or first thing in the morning? In other cases the insight might come to you after many months of consciously battling with a problem, with an 'incubation' period in between when you 'sleep on the problem'. Then again, in some cases your insight is a full-blown answer to a problem, with all the details, whereas in other cases it may be only the seed of an idea that needs further consideration. Or maybe a better *question* that takes you nearer to where you want to be. Many eureka experiences have changed lives and fortunes, and some the course of history. Chapter 2 gives some interesting examples.

The other aspect of peak performance is the experience of carrying out some activity over a period with complete ease, pleasure and mastery. This is often termed 'flow', or being 'in the zone' and is a more extended form of physical and mental 'high' than the eureka experience. Again, you will probably recognise at least some of the following.

➤ Sweeping through accumulated piles of work as if by magic the afternoon before leaving the office for a holiday.

➤ Those vital final strokes in a game of tennis, or critical scoring moments in any sport, when special forces seem to join you in your effortless brilliance.

➤ Scribbling down inspired chapters of your novel or pages of an important report you are writing, as words flood into your mind.

➤ The 'high' when jogging or doing other strenuous exercise when you pass through the pain barrier and enjoy an unexplained ecstatic state of mind.

➤ Those special yet unpredictable and inexplicable times in your hobby, job or pastime when things just cannot go wrong and you bask in the thrill of peak performance.

➤ A winning streak when you achieve best-ever results with seemingly no effort.

The important thing to understand about all these phenomena, right from the outset, is that they are common to all of us. Maybe one person gets more ideas than another person, and maybe one person's insight turns out to be more useful than another's. But each of us can cope with just about any job we 'put our mind to' and we are not dependent on our parents' genes or a super IQ.

Most exciting of all, the process can be *learned* — we can train our brains. However mystical these experiences may seem, there are things you can *do* as well as *know*. In this book you will learn ways to influence the number and quality of eureka and flow experiences you have to give you the special performance edge. These mental experiences, unusual or infrequent as they are, tend to bring out the *best* in you, and your consistent best will always achieve special results.

This is not to say that flashes and flow are the only factors involved in peak performance. Lots of other things play their part, from diet to Arcadian rhythms, and from height to financial inducements. In this book I have identified the two characteristics that I have found account for a *massive* part of all human excellence, and focused on these. The common features of creativity and intuition I address apply to every one of us and, even if latent, are within the potential of every reader. You will see from the next chapter that a single 'eureka' can have more effect than a three-month crash diet or fitness schedule, and a fifteen-minute period of 'flow' can have more effect on your performance than an eighteen-month training course. That's the reality. So it makes sense to go for what is universally applicable, has more or less unlimited potential for performance, and (unlike some approaches) can be supremely enjoyable.

FROM COMPETENCE TO EXCELLENCE

However random and accidental these experiences may be they are what can turn mediocre performance into excellence. They may not directly affect the job in hand, and it is more common for an idea or solution to come when your mind is on something else. But in the context of you as a total person, even apparently random insights will contribute to your achievement and success. Rather than the 1 or 2 per cent improvements you might get from linear, logical thinking (which computers can or will soon do better than us), intuitive, inductive thinking produces *quantum* advances. This is where breakthroughs come — the 'aha' insights, the memorable turning points in your life. At the same time the little ones, like remembering a name or where you have left something, the hint of a 'feeling' about a person or situation, or a subtle new angle on a problem that eventually brings the answer, all add up to effective, better performance.

For some people these experiences might occur hardly once a year. Stanley Kalms, the charismatic chairman of the Dixon's retail electrical chain, can receive half a dozen ideas out of the blue before arriving at the office in the morning. Keith Oates, deputy chairman of Marks and Spencer, is just as prolific, getting most of his ideas during the night. Sir Ralph Robins, chairman of Rolls-Royce, although not claiming any great quantity of eurekas, dates what turned out to be the biggest single engineering project in British history to a specific creative 'flow' session on a long aeroplane flight.

For some, these experiences bring mild pleasure and amusement, and possibly surprise, while others are lifted to ecstasy and a higher spiritual plane. One person looks on them as just a welcome bonus and others with curiosity, fascination and mystery. Many distrust and suppress anything that smacks of the mystical or non-rational. Some people seem devoid of imagination, and ideas, if they do come, are killed off at birth. Others almost depend on these experiences to cope with everyday problems and difficulties in business or other work, as well as for their overall personal achievement and career success. These are the people we usually admire as top performers in their field.

Inspiration of this sort is just about indispensable in the case of top leaders, whether in business, politics, the armed forces or any other field of activity — in fact wherever big problems, change and people are the order of the day. But top performers of all types, including in seemingly routine or physical activities, from manning a busy telephone switchboard to swimming for an Olympic gold medal, call on special mental resources to become the best at what they do. This creative, mental dimension — a sort of sixth-sense — seems to be the very stock in trade of human excellence. Sadly, dogged will power, careful planning and perseverance do not always bring about the goals many of us aspire to, whereas even a single good idea can sometimes change everything. And a few creative breakthroughs are enough to get anyone noticed, at whatever level in a job, hobby, sport or pastime. At worst, you will get more enjoyment out of whatever you put your hand to. More likely, tapping into your limitless creativity will be the single biggest factor in your success.

There will be no shortage of problems, but, using your whole brain, you can start to solve them with such confidence that you will almost welcome them. More positively, you can apply your innate creativity to spotting opportunities that you would otherwise have missed — and probably avoid many painful problems into the bargain. Once you know how to train your brain, you can apply it in any way you want to. You can advance your career, succeed in a self-employed capacity, learn a language, obtain a qualification, write a book or get to whatever level you feel capable of in your chosen sport, hobby or personal interests. Success is never all plain sailing, but even pressure and outside circumstances can be turned to your advantage (see Chapter 5) and — again by understanding and using your brain better — you can even make your own luck (Chapter 6). More than anything, *Train Your Brain* is about achieving your goals, and by tapping into your right brain resources you will start to harness your inbuilt goal-achieving mechanism. That is what turns mediocrity into excellence — consciously, habitually and pleasurably, achieving what you set out to achieve and being what you want to be.

Mixing and matching creative juices

Not surprisingly, these twin phenomena, although so different in many ways, are part of the same holistic mind-body system. They are interrelated and in practice overlap. For instance, an idea that comes to you 'out of the blue' can launch you into an extended period of high creativity and productivity. Sometimes ideas happen so quickly that it is difficult to write them down and a flow period starts, during which new lines of thinking are developed. In a similar way, a single motivating thought — some image, phrase or sensation — might spur an athlete to extraordinary performance, as if a special trigger had been released.

Alternatively, a period of flow is often interspersed with flashes of inspiration, sometimes in quick succession, which contribute to the extended 'high' and add to the overall impact. When achieving an important deadline at work, as well as the experience of flow which gives a sense of purpose, enjoyment and control over the task, you are likely to come up with ideas that are novel and unique. These ideas might then fuel your extended 'high'. Special reserves of physical energy allow you to carry on tirelessly, while mentally you are alert and creative, but without the usual grind of hard, conscious thinking.

So these two remarkable experiences, as well as drawing on the same unconscious mind, will readily invade each other's territory, but contribute none the less to the same outcome of special performance.

The jogger's high

Keen joggers describe special characteristics of the mental 'highs' that accompany the physical peaks and troughs of a run. In some cases they seem to break through to a higher mental plane, and in this state receive answers to problems and surprising insights that they would not have thought of 'in a thousand years' by effort and ordinary thinking processes. The benefits, for them, go well beyond the jogging experience. As well as a physical release valve, the jogging lifestyle habit is an outlet — in their case — for the unconscious mind. It can stimulate creativity and personal performance way beyond the time, distance and pulse measurements of the jog itself. The equivalent of the jogger's high crops up in many sports and physical activities. Physical and mental highs seem to work in harmony to help with real-life problems. Performance can pervade every area of your life. You can keep on doing what you like to do — creativity is associated with pleasure and relaxation — but get much more out of it. A lifestyle that is open to right brain insights (see Chapter 7) often attracts surprising bonuses.

Physical and mental highs

Physical and mental highs such as these are usually linked with times of special achievement and productivity; better *doing* comes with better *thinking*. The eureka itself may be linked with a physical sensation, as in the case of a 'gut feeling', about a person, say, or a business proposition, or the 'tingle factor' talked of in relation to a musical concert or when admiring a

great work of art. Emotion — always part of top performance — is literally a physical or moving experience. The performance 'zone' is physical, as in the case of a manual skill or a
fast sport when the mind seems to disengage altogether. Your
body is involved, but you perform on automatic pilot. This is part
of the way our mind-body system works.

On the other hand flow can be largely mental such as when
you are at your desk planning some change of systems and
hardly able to keep up with your prolific thoughts. There is a
flow of ideas rather than physical activity. Ideas, perhaps in the
shower or bath, or when driving or walking, evolve, develop and
build on each other as a continuous experience rather than a one
off eureka. Either way, your brain is the control centre of these
experiences, and that is where any training is best directed.

Use your imagination

Most of the above is a matter of common knowledge. But the
problem is that all too often it is relegated to serendipity, or some
mystical, creative talent someone else happens to have. So, for
most people, all this latent power stays under the bonnet and is
never transmitted into the super performance it was designed
for. In other cases intuition, when it surfaces, is suppressed or
explained away with reason.

Most people do recognise the importance of intuition, feelings and insights, even if for the most part they just admire them
in others. At worst, unsupported insights offer choices and
possibilities which you are free to follow or reject. At best they
transform a hopeless situation and lift you to amazing heights of
mental and physical excellence. So, imagine what would happen if you could *stimulate* these spontaneous insights and 'flow'
performance. Imagine they could increase in quality and usefulness as well as in quantity. Little further imagination is then
needed to make peak performance a personal reality. You can
start to recapture this precious childhood skill and use your
imagination to the full.

THE MIND-BODY PERFORMANCE PARTNERSHIP

Imagination? Mental powers? In fact everything you do and achieve involves both body and mind. For the body to operate at peak performance, the mind, whether consciously or unconsciously, is very much involved. In some situations, such as in some sports and manual activities, fitness and 'motor' skills are very important, but they are never the whole story. In the top league of just about any human activity, including seemingly physical activities, a large part of a person's success depends on mental skills, attitude and self-belief. Physical conditioning, although essential, is no more than a basic foundation upon which mental skills and attributes can build. Mental conditioning makes the critical difference. When a big financial or life-changing outcome hinges on a short sales presentation, interview or a critical snooker shot this fact becomes all too clear. Your mind might take over completely, however experienced or technically skilled you are. Suddenly we can become dithering incompetents or, conversely, masters of the moment. We usually do best when we just let go and get on with it.

Great soccer players are more often identified by their imagination, ingenuity or maybe 'genius' than for their physical prowess or purely technical skills, which can be too readily replicated by the competition. Golfers often claim that their game is 80 per cent mental and 20 per cent physical. Even apparently heavily 'physical' sports such as boxing, on close examination, are more to do with what is between the ears — not necessarily in a cerebral sense, but in terms of imagination, attitude, self-belief and a certain 'something'. But it starts in the mind. Our state of mind will influence even whether we are committed to physical practice or essential skill training. Thereafter it is a partnership of mind and body.

From thinking to doing

Just about every area of skill has its own version of that 'something' that makes the difference between mediocrity and excellence. Experts in self-development, as well as in management and professional work, speak of working smarter rather than harder, emphasising the importance of what goes on in the mind. Top business people tell of the importance of intuition and gut feelings, and trace their insights to real, bottom line results. You cannot excel at work if you leave your brain, or at least the creative part of it, at home. You cannot excel at anything without drawing on mental powers. These are not so much cerebral thinking powers, or intelligence, as your beliefs, attitudes and feelings. And these can be changed with the special kind of mental training I describe in this book. Mental resources then translate into performance. Thinking becomes doing, and doing brings achievement.

Divine choreography

The mind-body distinction, true as it is, is in danger of missing the crucial point. Peak performance involves not so much the mind and body as the mind-body — a single entity. There is no either/or. The late Formula 1 Grand Prix champion Ayrton Senna would sometimes describe a race in almost spiritual terms, in which he was at one with himself, the car and some seemingly outer power or force. He described what many other outstanding performers have done in their own way — a oneness of body, mind and purpose. This is what I have already described as being 'in the zone' or in a state of 'flow'. Masters in all sorts of activities — music, art, athletics — use their own words but refer to the same remarkable human experience. For some it is the inner glow of a job well done, for some the addictive satisfaction of being stretched and challenged, and for others the exhilaration of just being alive.

Often these experiences have a mystical or spiritual effect, and often defy logic, except, sometimes, with hindsight. During such times you may not be conscious of body, mind or anything about the activity you have mastered. So you can 'think' about your outcome or purpose rather than the mechanics of the immediate process. You can use your limited conscious mind to think tactically about your objective, or strategically about your higher outcomes, or to outsmart the competition. Or you can just savour the pleasure of the process, trusting your ability to succeed.

These are uniquely human experiences and one of the secrets of mastery and excellence in any activity or field of endeavour. They are the times when your mind and body seem divinely choreographed to achieve peak performance. Both experiences have to be understood to some degree, then respected and trusted to a fuller degree, before they become habitual and your performance can reach its peak.

ORCHESTRATED HARMONY

A mind-body partnership is always at work (or play). But the partnership goes further. The muscular, cardio-vascular and many other body 'systems' operate in amazing harmony. The master conducting happens in the brain which receives sensory feedback and instructs and controls physical movement, right down to a micro-muscular level. All this is too much for the conscious mind which can only think of a handful of things at one time, so the amazing job of orchestration happens unconsciously.

Success through symbiosis

Your brain, however, is not just concerned with coordinating physical functions and movement, but with problems, feelings and making choices. Much of this happens intuitively. And, as with deep-rooted self-beliefs, attitudes and irrational feelings, and habitual, 'autopilot' activities, it is beyond your conscious rational thinking. Either way, what goes on in the brain, whether by way of attitude, temperament or state of mind, and desire, will be — or should be, for top performance — in harmony with every cell in your body. Each set of mind systems serves corresponding body systems, and vice versa. So your state of mind can instantly affect every part of your physiology — muscles, breathing, blood pressure, strength, colour etc. What you think about your teenage daughter not being home when expected, whether based on logic or emotion, will affect your blood pressure, body chemistry and the hundreds of muscle movements that go to make up your change in physiology. Conversely what happens in your body will instantly affect your mind in a circular or symbiotic way. Hence the common dilemma, 'Do I whistle because I am happy or am I happy because I whistle?' Usually this complex two-way process happens without any conscious interference on your part, and that's the way it should be. The kind of intelligence that translates into achievement is more emotional than cerebral, and emotion involves body as well as mind. 'Gut feelings' are beginning to get the respect they deserve.

Inter-brain teamwork

Moreover, one part of your mind affects another. For example, a logical thought might be overridden by an intuition, or 'common sense'. Conversely, an intuitive idea might be tested and tempered with logical, rational thoughts. You may well be 'in two minds'. And this can affect your performance; as long as there is a lack of harmony and indecision you will be operating below par. Equivocation can be disastrous in high pressure business dealings, or when you have to nip in the bud an interpersonal relationship problem. But it is just as apparent at the critical points in a tennis match or in many other sports requiring rhythm and coordination. We do things best that come *naturally*. When your two minds — logical and intuitive — and all their systems, are in harmony you will begin to achieve peak performance. In many cases this requires a team effort, but here, in fact, is where real teamwork happens. When the mind-body team, and its multitude of mental and physical members, is headed in one direction you become unstoppable and unbeatable. You perform at your best.

Physically, your two brain hemispheres are separate and more or less identical, but operate in completely different ways. Simplified for our immediate purpose, one side is adept at language and logic, and the other at intuition, feelings and creative imagining. Consciously, you might rightly say 'I'm in two minds' or 'My mind (left brain) says this but my heart (right brain, or limbic system) says the other'. And these common experiences reflect the literal two-mind reality. However, each brain hemisphere is linked by a couple of hundred million fibres in the form of the corpus callosum, like an information super highway, so there is ample provision for communication between them. And this inter-brain dialogue produces optimal thinking and performance. At worst, these different ways of thinking generate options — choices. If you harness them the quality of your resulting behaviour can only get better.

Heart and mind

Harmony between the parts of your body involves the thousands of electro-chemical muscular and other activities that go to make up what we term a skill, mastery or super performance. Harmony in the mind involves two very different parts of the brain, at least in terms of the way we think — the software or the rational, logical side, and the intuitive, imaginative and often unconscious side. The final partnership of mind and body then creates the seemingly superhuman performance that we aspire to. Such a degree of neurophysiological orchestration is rare, but this is more due to ignorance and educational conditioning than genetic short-changing. When there is harmony between 'heart and mind', it means that mind and body are also at one. Positive, empowering emotions are the physical side of the mind-body handshake. At times of special performance the critical left brain lets the childlike, imaginative right brain perform the skills it does naturally, and starts to trust the insights it receives from the deep oceans of the subconscious. That is the essence of peak performance.

Fortunately to operate at peak performance you do not have to understand these fantastic mind-body functions that make up perhaps 90 per cent of all your behaviour and underpin even the most basic skill. But you do need to have a level of trust in what is possible, and especially an appreciation of the extent to which much of what happens happens unconsciously. So you don't have to know how you do what you do well, but you need to know you can do it. This kind of trust and apparent loss of control is hard for many active, intelligent people to accept. So some humility is called for, but that has always been a characteristic of true masters.

UNCONSCIOUS COMPETENCE

Peak performance is an holistic, body-mind experience. It usually combines clear, creative thinking and skill, with dexterity and economy of physical effort, in different degrees. Although attained over a period by effort and practice, of which we are very much conscious, top performance — at the time we are actually engaged in the activity or skill — is characterised by unconscious competence. The process is automatic — so much so that even world experts can often not find words to describe what they do that produces their outstanding results. Quite simply, they do not think about it, so they do not know, any more than a skilled coach or spectator really knows. It happens largely unconsciously.

Unconscious competence is one of the keys to peak performance, but again is not the whole story. The conscious mind is concerned both in learning and perfecting the activity. Sometimes this is a long and arduous process, involving trial and error, setbacks and frustration, self-discipline and commitment. And this is just as common, or even more so, in top performers such as Olympic competitors or world champions as is the state of 'flow' or 'not trying'. So just as we cannot separate mind and body in the quest for performance, nor can we attribute it either to the conscious or unconscious part of the mind. Different mental systems are at work all the time, and each produces its best in different situations and at different times.

When it comes to our attempts to improve performance there is usually no shortage of conscious effort — of trying. In many cases there is discipline and commitment, sweat and tears. But this is where there may be some unlearning to do and we may have to redress the balance towards more spontaneous, 'auto-pilot' skills. That means you may actually have to stop trying, which for some people is the hardest part of all. Competence can only become excellence when we stop trying, and are not even conscious of our skill. A major research study concluded that an astonishing 99 per cent of all our learning is unconscious. But this reflects in the fact that almost all our behaviour is carried out unconsciously — governed by habit — including the most complex activities and skills. Unconscious competence is a major feature of peak performance.

MYTHS AND MISUNDERSTANDINGS

The human mind has always been shrouded in mystique and controversy. At best there are usually some basic questions that have to be addressed to remove unnecessary obstacles to learning, and to foster a reasonably open mind. Here are some typical questions I encounter.

Is my brain up to it?

With all the recent scientific advances in the area of the human brain, many of the whys remain. But the breakthrough, from which we can all benefit, is in knowing how we can harness this resource to bring about specific outcomes. As far as most researchers are concerned, the potential of the human brain is, to all intents and purposes, unlimited. The evidence for this, whether through rigorous research or centuries of anecdote, is overwhelming. Yes, your brain is well up to it. And reading this book will bring this fantastic power within your practical grasp. You already have the innate resources, although they may well be latent, and almost certainly are not being used to their full potential. Chapter 3 says a lot more about your brain resources and how you can tap them for different purposes.

Is this for anybody?

The phenomena I have described are not confined to special, famous people. Some of the well-known historical figures mentioned in the next chapter might hardly be remembered today if these 'gifts from the gods', as they have been referred to, had not occurred. That is, rather than receiving such mental gifts because they were special, they are famous because they trusted and acted on their eurekas. Indeed the very randomness and unconsciousness of the process renders the highest intellect and most impressive qualifications of little use. In some cases an analytical mind, or any sort of mental effort, can be counterproductive, and actually block creativity. Trying harder doesn't necessarily work. This is the point: we all have a more or less standard brain. It's the way we use it — or perhaps the way we let it use us — that determines our thoughts and achievements. So when it comes to using our 3½lb. standard issue ration of grey matter the playing fields are level. All this creative brainpower, and the performance that follows, is within the reach of ordinary people.

Nature or nurture?

Where do hereditary factors figure in this? If heredity is at work, it is an insignificant factor — especially if, as some experts contend, we use such a tiny part of our brains in the first place. And, in any event, these factors can easily be outbalanced by how you think and what you do now. Choices are always there to be found, and choices mean you can change and have more control. You need not be a slave to either fortune or heredity. You can think what you want to think, and adopt the lifestyle you want to adopt and so harness all this performance power in your life. Your freedom to pursue chosen goals, as we shall see, is greater than any nature or nurture influence. Although the rules are different, there are things you can do consciously to foster unconscious thinking processes. It is not so much a matter of will power, self-discipline, or IQ, as of imagination and intuition, the currency of the right side of the brain. Metaphorically, although you cannot produce the fruit, and unconscious habits will continue unconsciously, you can sow the seed and prepare the ground for unconscious competence. This special mental and physical preparation is covered in Chapter 7. Genetics are secondary to simple lifestyle changes you can decide positively about. One by one, you can change disempowering habits and undo what vestiges of nature might prevent you from rising to your full potential.

Can I be trained for peak performance?

Yes, you can train the unconscious part of the brain, but not in the same way you train for conscious skills. To start with, it is not at home with words and numbers. In addition, the moment you stop thinking about what you are doing, habits take over. That is just the way we function. So these habits have got to be right, and self-beliefs may have to be changed first. To achieve this sort of change, the learning process, described in Chapter 7, is different.

Spontaneous idea generation or skill 'flow' is more associated with the right side of the brain, where imagery, intuition and feelings, rather than language and logic, are the raw material. It is the world of dreaming and daydreaming, of incubating, or sleeping on a problem, and of all the flashes of inspiration that seem to defy logic. This is not to say, however, that you cannot influence this side of your thinking. For a start — and this is well borne out by experience — you are more likely to get these experiences when you are relaxed and not consciously thinking about anything in particular, such as when showering or commuting to work. And it follows that a lifestyle that excludes personal 'space', times of winding down, or running in neutral thinking gear, will suppress such subtle processes.

Fortunately, lifestyle can be changed, although not in the way that we learn specific knowledge and skills. It is just a collection of habits, and these can be changed using the kind of techniques NLP (neuro-linguistic programming) provides, and which I describe in Chapter 7. So change, at this basic lifestyle level, is within your control. The huge potential of operating at peak performance makes the simple changes I suggest a first-class investment.

You can further promote creative thinking through controlling your state of mind at the time and in the situations you need to, and again there are simple models you will learn. Creative thinking is a learnable process. And we are all natural learners, as well as natural achievers. All the benefits are within your reach. Approached in the way I set out in this book it is as accessible as learning a new language, a special cake recipe or crown green bowling, but the benefits apply far more widely. You can learn how to learn or how to activate unconscious learning. Learning how to catch fish is better than being given fish. Learning how to learn is better than learning how to fish. It is about training your brain, and this is one of the secrets of excellence.

Is it for work or personal achievement?

These intuitive skills need not be confined to your work or any single part of your life. What happens in the case of the Nobel prize-winning scientist is much the same as for the writer, entrepreneur, nurse, cabinet maker or tennis player. Descriptions about creativity and intuition are uncannily familiar to most people, even though the consequences may not all be as earth-shattering. That is because we operate at different levels of influence. You may be responsible for a budget of £10 or £1 million, run a global corporation or just look after your own back garden. But the conditions under which creativity seems to flourish, and the characteristics of eureka and flow experiences, when investigated, turn out to be almost standard.

It is a sad fact, therefore, that the average worker leaves his or her creative brain in the company car park each morning. Individuals who display remarkable creativity in their chosen hobby, sport or weekend pursuits, are usually very different at work, where the organisation structure, systems and culture may not encourage risk taking or new ideas. For other people the reverse is true and they seem to enjoy their performance 'highs' when at work. A truly creative writer may not associate her creativity with solving everyday problems at home or reordering the filing system. And a highly ingenious mother and housewife may not use her right brain skills for the good of her employer where the culture may not be supportive. Any creativity we display is likely to have developed as an accidental result of our family background, education or early career, and tends to be confined to just a part of a person's life. In very few cases do we actively develop and extend our creativity as we might other skills. But, however our imagination has been allowed to atrophy, we are all naturally creative, and this usually surfaces, more often than not, in a hobby or other non-work activity. With the 'reframing' techniques you will meet in Chapter 8 you can start to extend this natural creativity to other parts of your life.

WHAT'S IN IT FOR ME?

It is hard indeed to think of any area of work or personal life that might not benefit from a bit of new, original thinking. The idea of continuous quality, or Kaizan (the Japanese term for the concept of continous improvement as applied, e.g., in quality circles) although all too often paid mere lip service on the part of company bosses, depends on a continuous stream of creative thinking. The process is dynamic and demands insight at every stage, right up to successful implementation of change. Logic is not enough. Almost by definition, logical improvements would have been thought of a long time ago, as so much thought has already gone into the problems. Something more is needed, and this is the dimension of thinking that produces the strange anecdotes you will read in the next chapter. Once tapped, it can be used in any situation. Your creative brain has no favourite subjects other than what you believe is important and worth while. It will happily follow your agenda, even when you have not articulated what you want or when you are sound asleep. Because it can be harnessed, you can choose which areas of your life would benefit from creative insight and in what order of priority. You can intervene into what is otherwise an unconscious process.

Here are some situations in which you can benefit from these unconscious insights and ideas.

You want to achieve more with less effort

One characteristic of this sort of thinking is that you do not really need to think in the sense that we usually use the term. Effort is minimal or non-existent. Instead of the marginal or diminishing returns you get when working hard at a problem, the returns are not usually related to your inputs, at least in any identifiable way. It turns out there is more effort involved in arriving at a mediocre solution by logical methods than in arriving at a much better solution through insight or inspiration. And the effort involved in just about any activity is eliminated when you are in a state of mental and physical flow.

This does not mean that top performance does not require effort, such as in implementing an idea or practising a physical skill. To start with, there is a time to train and practice, and a time to let go and play the real game. A smarter, more creative approach also means that your effort is not wasted but directed into real achievement, and based on quality decisions. You won't be banging your head against metaphorical brick walls or spinning your metaphorical wheels. More to the point practically, it means that the effort doesn't seem like work because of the pleasure you get in the process and subsequent achievements. Effort in peak performance is optimal effort — there is a right level. But as a rule it takes more effort to fail than to succeed.

You feel you are not fulfilling your true potential

This is all too common, and is frustrating if you are exerting effort and energy conscientiously and have a genuine desire to succeed. Sometimes overall direction is missing, but in other cases a bit of insight, luck or serendipity — the odd 'leg up' or 'shot in the arm' — is all you need. That is what intuition and flow are all about. But by using in effect one half of your brain — the logical, rational side — it is a simple neurological fact that you will not achieve your full potential. It is just as obvious where to concentrate if you want to achieve your best.

You have to tackle big problems

Logical thinking processes can maybe cope with problems that have a single, acceptable logical solution. Most real problems, however, do not fit that neat requirement, especially those concerning people. Sometimes you can't even define the problem. In any event, the increasing power and sophistication of computers means that once you can express a problem in a linear, logical way the task can be delegated to a machine — and that is not the stuff of the human imagination. Your problem-solving ability is in an entirely different league. It is therefore not surprising that the mental process that produces uniquely human insights, feelings and imagination are associated with the right, non-rational brain. The process is an holistic, parallel rather than linear one. Your right brain does what it does in a different way, and because this is the unconscious part of your mind, and does not use the language of words and symbols, in a way that you cannot begin to understand. As with dreams, maybe you are not meant to. But, as we shall see clearly in the next chapter, no problem is too big for the human imagination. The 'problem' is that we often do not appreciate our innate thinking powers or trust the ideas that bubble up to the surface. Start trusting your brain resources, and you will soon start to value and trust what it hands over to your conscious mind.

You want to make up lost time and achieve past dreams

Although seeming effortless at the time they occur, spontaneous insights are often so dramatic in their impact that they can bring about change that ordinary thinking through of the problem would not produce. Deep-seated mindsets are disturbed. It affects our feelings as well as our intellect. Attitudes and beliefs may also be involved, not just pros and cons and a measured, cerebral response. But all these insights or revelations help us achieve some outcome or purpose. Inspiration does not happen without a meaning, even though we may not recognise the meaning at the moment of revelation. Sometimes, indeed, the hoped-for outcome is just to get out of a mess, respond to a crisis or survive. But the principle is the same. If your house is due to be repossessed on Friday week you suddenly become very creative and entertain ideas that would not have previously 'entered you mind'. But whether positive or negative, your outcomes are expertly serviced by your unconscious mind in the form of associations, ideas, visualised scenarios and the odd eureka. Once the process is understood and trusted, dreams or goals that have so far eluded you can be quickly realised. Huge brain resources, hitherto latent and unused, can be harnessed in pursuit of your outcomes. And the power of the goal-achieving imagination is such that age, genetic pedigree and all manner of negative circumstances need be no obstacle. So dreams that have lain dormant for a long time can be within your reach.

You want to leave your mark

You may want to make an impact in a career or sport, in a work of art or literature, or in some contribution to society or your family that will long outlive you. Time after time the lasting effect of individuals on their immediate world, or even the whole human race, are traced back to spontaneous insights and mysterious times of flow. Even when the breakthroughs come from long, hard discipline and effort, the process is invariably kept going by occasional special insights that lift the research or endeavour to a higher plane of knowledge or achievement. We need the odd shot in the arm if we are to produce something memorable. It seems doubtful whether any true progress would be made if people did not draw on their intuitive mind.

You want to enjoy what you do

Pleasure is one of the recurring characteristics of this kind of thinking. With conscious, left brain problem solving you can almost feel the cogs turning. It sometimes hurts. A right brain intuition, on the other hand, is like the extra special little complimentary dish the chef serves — a pleasant surprise, easy to digest and it comes ready to eat 'on a plate'. Whatever important desires these insights address, the process is a happy one. And, strangely, there can also be pleasure even when the issues being thought about are not in themselves pleasant.

One business executive had an important and rather unpleasant decision to make regarding a senior member of his staff. After tormenting himself with the many factors for some time he woke up one Friday morning completely certain of which way to go. Although he still had to carry out some distasteful actions, he had an uncanny sense of relief at having finally come to a decision. The difficult part, he felt, was over. And his pleasure was in the knowledge that the right solution had come to him, and the sense of calm certainty he had about such a sensitive matter. The decision, he insisted, had been made for him. Intuition knows without knowing where the knowledge came from. It knows without knowing how it knows. There is great pleasure in knowing that you have access to your full thinking power and in the peak performance that it enables.

As you read the remarkable stories in the next chapter, try to spot from the quotes the pleasure factor, and other conditions, circumstances and clues, as to how you can draw more on your amazing brain powers.

WHAT'S IN *TRAIN YOUR BRAIN*?

This book will give you all the information and skills you will need to perform at your best. In this chapter I have described the two phenomena that will give you the edge in personal performance and explained the mind-body partnership. Having disposed of a few common questions we have also seen the direct benefits of increasing, in quality and quality, these flash and flow experiences. The rest of the book will show how you can translate this knowledge into skills, ideas and achievements so that you can operate at peak performance.

This will require not just head knowledge but a level of trust in your own unconscious mind before consistent high performance is reached. You need to open your mind to possibilities so that you do not limit yourself. The following chapter tells a more comprehensive story of brain training as it has affected science, business and individual lives in dramatic ways. This will illustrate, from the lives of real people, the variety and value of these creative experiences we all can enjoy. But these are not just stories; the anecdotes contain the vital principles upon which you and I can base our performance, and suggest the circumstances (many of which we can create) that will enhance your creativity and achievement. In Chapter 4 I draw these out, helping you to relate even well-known historic events to your own experience and circumstances, but after concentrating first in Chapter 3 on the fantastic brain, and how you can stimulate it for top performance. This understanding will add further to your trust in your own mind-body resources. Chapter 5 shows how you can turn pressure, with which we are all familiar, into positive performance. In Chapter 6 you will learn how to create your own luck. Then Chapter 7 describes how you can get into the right state of mind for creativity and super 'flow' performance, and, if necessary, to change limiting self-beliefs. This chapter includes, for example, techniques for relaxing and tips about lifestyle. Chapter 8 describes specific techniques you can use to stimulate creativity, solve problems and apply your new understanding, belief and confidence to exceed in whatever you do. In the final chapter I suggest a three-week brain training action schedule that will transform your learning into something exceptional.

2

WORLD-CHANGING CREATIVITY

History is full of examples of extraordinary individual creativity that has changed lives and whole societies. Recent years have, if anything, been even more prolific in intuitive flashes and flow as the pace of learning and invention has increased. Time after time spontaneous ideas are transformed into world-class performance in science, music, literature, sport, business and every walk of life. The better-known cases we look at in this chapter are often associated with genius. In some cases the impact of a single insight many decades ago, such as the discovery of penicillin or the anti-polio vaccine, or the invention of the transistor or the microwave oven, has a unique effect on all our lives today. The examples in this chapter will show just how widespread the phenomenon is, and will help you to relate special creativity to your own experience. These real-life anecdotes also give clues about the characteristics of intuitive thinking and lessons you can apply to improve your own performance. I draw together these lessons in Chapter 4, but for the moment watch out for common features that you might be able to reproduce in your own experience and tips you can immediately apply.

THE MYTH OF SCIENTIFIC METHOD

Apart from Archimedes' bathtub 'eureka', perhaps the best-known example from the world of science in the early twentieth century is Einstein — all the more remarkable in that as a mathematician he dealt very much in logical, 'left brain' matters. From the time he was sixteen he puzzled over what would happen if someone tried to capture a ray of light.

$$e = mc^2$$

On one occasion, according to several published accounts, Einstein daydreamed he was riding on a beam of light that he followed in his mind's eye back to its point of origin. He then proceeded to formulate the mathematical equations that would support his intuitive knowledge, and elevate his childlike dream to one of the most famous theories in the history of science — the theory of relativity and the equation of equations $e = mc^2$. It is well known that Einstein placed a high value on his intuition. He wrote: 'The intellect has little to do on the road to discovery. There comes a leap in consciousness, call it intuition or what you will, and the solution comes to you and you don't know how or why.' And on another occasion: 'To raise new questions, new possibilities, to regard old problems from a new angle, requires creative imagination, and marks real advance in science.' There is not much reference here to rational, scientific method.

Einstein illustrates not just that intuition is compatible with, and even endemic in, scientific research, but also our practical dependence on it for any worthwhile achievement, however far fetched an idea seems. In his case his intuitive imagination ran a long way ahead of current knowledge, so was ripe for rubbishing by any critical, rational thinker. In this sense, at least, things have changed little for creative thinkers over the years.

Muscles of intuition

Sir Isaac Newton also worked out his proofs and conducted his experiments to verify what he had first determined intuitively. Newton is ranked as one of the foremost rationalists of the seventeenth century's Age of Reason, yet, paradoxically to some, was also one of the most intuitive of Western scientists. Economist John Maynard Keynes, in an essay about Newton, referred to his 'muscles of intuition'. He was also described as 'so happy in his conjectures as to seem to know more than he could possibly have a means of proving'.

The famous DNA double helix

The key moment in the search for the structure of the DNA molecule in the 1950s came when co-discoverer James Watson was manipulating the components of a model molecule, trying to fit them together in different ways. He and his research partner, Francis Crick, had always assumed, as had other scientists, that each segment had to be paired with its twin. Watson suddenly became aware 'that both pairs could be flip-flopped and still have their ... bonds facing the same direction. It strongly suggested that the backbones of the two chains run in opposite directions.'

That instantaneous realisation triggered the discovery of the famous DNA double helix. It is hard to overstate the major role of intuition in scientific and technological advances.

The benzene ring

The chemist Kekulé, in the nineteenth century, who discovered the molecular structure of benzene, described a dream-like experience. This is typical of the creative process, yet again was extraordinary in its impact on science. Until that time all known chemical structures were composed of linear chains of atoms, and like other chemists of his time Kekulé had tried in vain to fit the six carbon atoms and six hydrogen atoms of benzene into a chain that satisfied the rules of chemistry. One night, after a good meal and a couple of glasses of brandy, he settled down to relax by the open fire. Half asleep, he watched the flames twisting and curling upon themselves, and in his mind they seemed like snakes circling round to bite their own tails. He woke up with a start. 'Flames do not go round in circles', he pondered, 'but carbon atoms in the benzene molecule could'. It was a closed chain, a ring structure. In a way Kekulé already 'knew' the answer. But his belief that it must be in the form of a chain was blocking him. Only when he took his mind completely off the task could his unconscious speak to him and show him what it knew. As is often the case it spoke in the language of the unconscious, in images and dreams.

The cases of Einstein, Watson and Kekulé were major scientific breakthroughs. A lot that had gone before and was accepted as true was brought together in a new synthesis — and it is this synthesis that makes some insights so special. What occurred has been described as a paradigm change. Although few examples of inspiration fall into this paradigm category, the process is the same. The difference is that a lot more (in some cases hundreds of years') knowledge was synthesised, so the effect was so much more startling. In Einstein's case, mathematical rules and processes had to catch up with the greater truth of the creative insight. When right and left brain work in harmony we begin to produce peak performance.

MIND OVER MATHEMATICS

The logical world of mathematics is an alien place for unsupported hunches and intuition. The famous mathematician Poincaré, however, gives his own memorable account in the early years of the twentieth century of the same sort of inexplicable phenomenon that resulted in a historic mathematical breakthrough.

The Fuchsian function phenomenon

Poincaré writes:

> *For fifteen days I strove to prove that there could not be any functions like those I have since called Fuchsian functions. I was then very ignorant; every day I seated myself at my work table, stayed an hour or two, tried a great number of combinations and reached no results. One evening, contrary to my custom, I drank black coffee and could not sleep. Ideas rose in crowds; I felt them collide until pairs interlocked, so to speak, making a stable combination. By the next morning I had established the existence of a class of Fuchsian functions, those which came from the hypergeometric series; I had only to write out the results, which took but a few hours.*

'On the bus'

Poincaré then worked on his ideas in a conscious and deliberate way, and later describes another remarkable moment:

> *The changes of travel [he was on a geological excursion] made me forget my mathematical work. Having reached Coutances, we entered an omnibus to go to some place or other. At the moment when I put my foot on the step the idea came to me, without anything in my former thoughts seeming to have paved the way for it, that the transformations I had used to define the Fuchsian functions were identical with those of non-Euclidean geometry. I did not verify the idea; I should not have had time, as, upon taking my seat in the omnibus, I continued with a conversation already commenced, but I felt a perfect certainty. On my return to Caen, for conscience sake, I verified the result at my leisure.*

'At the seaside'

Again he embarked on some arithmetical questions 'without much success and without a suspicion of any connection with my preceding researches'. Disgusted with his failure, he went to spend a few days at the seaside, and thought of other things. Then he continues:

> *One morning, walking on the bluff, the idea came to me, with just the same characteristics of brevity, suddenness and immediate certainty, that the arithmetic transformation of indeterminate ternary quadratic forms were identical with those of non-Euclidean geometry.*

'Walking along the street'

Still more systematic, conscious work followed. Still he encountered more difficulties and frustration. He then moved to Mont-Valerien, where he was to go through military service, so was very differently occupied. And once again, the eureka phenomenon:

> *One day, going along the street, the solution of the difficulty which had stopped me suddenly appeared to me. I did not try to go deep into it immediately, and only after my service did I again take up the question. I had all the elements and had only to arrange them and put them together. So I wrote out my final memoir at a single stroke and without difficulty.*

Poincaré's experience is by no means untypical, and his descriptions — at the seaside, on the bus, walking along the street — have a familiar ring. The only unusual thing about his accounts is the succession of such revelations contributing to the eventual historical breakthrough, although even these happened over a longish period. He seems to have developed a lifestyle of creativity and the habit of intuition. In his case the impact was great, at least in the world of mathematics. But even in the occasional brainwaves most people experience, the impact on the person involved may be no less than Poincaré's. In some cases, while leaving no impression on the wider world, such an experience can well change a person's life. The examples you and I can quote may be less significant, but none the less remarkable in the mysterious, surprising way in which they occur, and the pleasure they bring in solving a problem or opening up an important opportunity.

THE CREATIVE POWER OF WORDS

Writers over the centuries have had a close relationship with the Muse, crediting their ideas and even the words they write, to an outside source. But the characteristics of these unusual experiences which have had such a great effect on our literature and culture turn out to be the same as for great scientific breakthroughs. Each, in its own way, has changed the course of history and affects each of our lives today.

Who wrote *Jonathan Livingston Seagull?*

After *Jonathan Livingston Seagull* became a bestseller, author Richard Bach used to startle interviewers by announcing: 'I didn't write it.' Asked who did, he would explain how he was walking alone along the waterfront in Long Beach, California one evening when he heard a voice call out: 'Jonathan Livingston Seagull'. He felt that he had experienced something of special significance. But he was a novice writer and didn't even have a typewriter. So scribbling rapidly in longhand on a yellow pad, he finished the first part of the story in one sitting. Eleanor Friede, the book's editor, says Bach told her it was as if he were watching a movie. He saw this bird flying and wrote what he saw. Nothing had ever come to him that way before. Then suddenly the movie stopped and he had to stop writing. The movie didn't start up again for six years. But one day he woke at three o'clock in the morning and the movie was running in his head again. He got up, went to the typewriter he owned by then, and finished the story. Bach still maintains that he didn't write the book but that it merely came 'through' him.

Thinking about nothing in particular

The poet A. E. Housman described how his own verses often arose in his mind:

> *As I went along, thinking of nothing in particular, only looking at things around me and following the progress of the seasons, there would flow into my mind, with sudden and unaccountable emotion, sometimes a line or two of a verse, sometimes a whole stanza at once, accompanied, not preceded, by a vague notion of the poem which they were destined to form part of. Then there would usually be a lull of an hour or so and the spring would bubble again.*

Inspiration may be little more than the seed of an idea, and very incomplete, but then there is the experience of flow, in which one idea follows another, like a bubbling spring, and a pattern or whole emerges.

MUSIC IN THE MIND

Here is a quote that illustrates some of the characteristics of spontaneous creative thinking I look at in Chapter 4, but this time in the world of music.

'entirely alone ... of good cheer'

When I am, as it were, completely myself, entirely alone, and of good cheer — say travelling in a carriage, or walking after a good meal, or during the night when I cannot sleep; it is on such occasions that my ideas flow best and most abundantly. Whence and how *[his emphasis]* they come, I know not; nor can I force them. This pleasure that pleases me I retain in my memory, and am accustomed, as I have been told, to hum them to myself. If I continue in this way, it soon occurs to me how I may turn this or that morsel to account, so as to make a good dish of it, that is to say, agreeably to the rules of counterpoint, to the peculiarities of the various instruments, etc.

'fires my soul'

All this fires my soul, and, provided I am not disturbed, my subject enlarges itself, becomes methodised and defined, and the whole, though it be long, stand as almost complete and finished in my mind, so that I can survey it, like a fine picture or a beautiful statue, at a glance. Nor do I hear in my mind the parts successively, but I hear them, as it were, all at once. What a delight this is I cannot tell! All this inventing, this producing, takes place in a pleasing lively dream. Still the actual hearing of the tout ensemble is after all the best. What has been thus produced I do not easy forget, and this is perhaps the best gift I have the Divine Maker to thank for. When I proceed to write down my ideas, I take out of the bag of my memory, if I may use that phrase, what has previously been collected into it in the way I have mentioned.

'committing to paper'

For this reason the committing to paper is done quickly enough, for everything is, as I have said before, already finished; and it rarely differs on paper from what it was in my imagination. At this occupation I can therefore suffer myself to be disturbed; for whatever is going on around me, I write, and even talk, but only of fowls and geese, or of Gretel or Barbel, or some such matters, But why my productions take from my hand that particular form and style that makes them Mozartish, and different from the works of other composers, is probably owing to the same *cause which renders my nose so large or aquiline, or, in short, makes it Mozart's, and different from those of other people. For I really do not study or aim for originality.*

As you will have gathered, those were the words of the great composer Mozart. Another great composer says something very similar:

'suddenly and unexpectedly'

Generally speaking, the germ of a future composition comes suddenly and unexpectedly. If the soil is ready — that is to say, if the disposition for work is there — it takes root with extraordinary force and rapidity, shoots up through the earth, puts forth branches, leaves and finally, blossoms. I cannot define the creative process by any other way than by this simile. The great difficulty is that the germ must appear at a favourable moment, the rest goes of itself. It would be vain to put into words that immeasurable sense of bliss which comes over me directly a new idea awakens in me and begins to assume a definite form. I forget everything and behave like a madman. Everything within me starts pulsing and quivering; hardly have I begun to sketch ere one thought follows another.

Above are the words of the composer Tchaikovsky. He then says something which shows the awesome power of inspiration: 'If that condition of mind and soul which we call inspiration, lasted long without intermission, no artist could survive it. The strings would break and the instrument be shattered into fragments.' Some of his other accounts give us more clues about the nature of this intuitive experience, and lessons we can learn.

'Bliss', 'magic', 'inspiration', 'a supernatural and inexplicable force' — and all without racking the brain. This is human creativity at work and the key to peak performance.

The phenomenon is so common among artists and writers, whether famous or unknown, that we hardy need to quote examples. Such people are usually associated with special creativity. But the characteristics are the same as for scientists, businesspeople, students, sportspeople and accountants, whatever the stereotype. The businessman who woke during the night with a ready-made report gave a very similar description to Mozart and Tchaikovsky. In each case purposes were fulfilled, problems solved and ideas turned into reality. Peak performance was attained.

IDEAS THAT CHANGED LIVES

The stereotype inventor is as right brained as the musician and artist, so it is no surprise that the history of inventions is a history of creative thinking and specifically of eureka type inspiration. Useful innovations require more than raw creativity, however, as is nicely overstated in Edison's famous quotation: '1 per cent inspiration, 99 per cent perspiration'.

The fact remains, however, that the breakthroughs usually came in characteristic flash form, however long and laborious the search. And the breakthroughs and paradigm changes are what made the big lasting difference. I am not concerned here about dreams that remain dreams or crazy inventions that never became reality. That's creativity without innovation or utility. You can soon check the power of the imagination by looking around you at the things you take for granted and which were once only a bubble rising from somebody's imagination. The world is full of inventions that started out as crazy dreams.

Instant insight

Edwin Land, out of whose intuition came non-glare Polaroid glass, instant film and the instant camera, maintained that every significant step in every field ' is taken by some individual who has freed himself from a way of thinking that is held by friends and associates who may be more intelligent, better educated, better disciplined, but who have not mastered the art of the fresh, clean look at old, old knowledge.'

Bookmarks and blood analysers

Inventor Art Fry of 3M was singing in a choir and needed bookmarks that wouldn't fall out of his hymnal when he got the idea for Post-It notes, those ubiquitous little yellow memos with a strip of adhesive on the back.

John J. Moran, a onetime lab technician, made a fortune by inventing an automatic blood analyser in 1965. For months he had worked unsuccessfully trying to design the machine. Finally, in frustration, he embarked on a long-postponed holiday. On his first day away, as the sun's rays filtered through the hotel room window on to his face, he saw in his mind's eye a detailed picture of the machine. He sprang from his bed, hastily sketched a diagram on hotel note paper, and flew home, spending the next few months building the prototype from the sketch. The prototype worked perfectly, and in 1979 he sold out to a German company for $40 million. The crucial idea came free, which is an appealing aspect of spontaneous creative thinking.

Spears and sewing machines

Although an earlier case I referred to occurred in the middle of the night I have not yet mentioned the role of dreams. These cases can be even more remarkable. One such concerns Elias Howe, the inventor of the sewing machine. He had laboured for several years and was one small detail away from his goal. Then one night he dreamed he had been captured by a tribe of savages whose leader had commanded him to finish his machine or else he would be killed. In the dream, the terrified inventor was surrounded by warriors leading him to his death, when he suddenly noticed that his captors' spears had eye-shaped holes near the points. Howe woke from his dream and whittled a model of a needle with the hole near the point instead of in the middle of the shank as in earlier experiments. The change was the key to completing a workable sewing machine.

Inventions that beat the experts

Intuitive creativity is a great leveller and does not respect conventional learning, IQ or qualifications. An analysis of fifty-eight major twentieth-century inventions, from chemicals to computers to ball-point pens, reveals that in forty-six of those discoveries the inventor was an individual, a small firm or somebody in the 'wrong business'. King Gillette, the inventor of the safety razor, was a cork salesman. George Eastman, when he revolutionised photography, was a bookkeeper, while a couple of musicians invented Kodachrome. John Dunlop, co-inventor of the pneumatic tyre, was a vet. The automatic telephone system was invented by an undertaker, and a watch-maker trying to solve a brass fitting problem came up with continuous casting steel. The soap makers ignored detergents, and the dye makers invented them instead, while the aircraft engine manufacturers repeatedly spurned the jet engine, leaving its development to the airframe makers. A seat-of-the-pants combat pilot returned from Vietnam with the overnight Federal Express system tucked away in his head and went on to beat the US postal service at its own business, creating one of the fastest growth corporations in history. So much for the experts. When it comes to creative thinking, a fertile mind is worth a string of academic degrees or even years of experience.

Inventions that cause conflict

Intuitive thinking is often at odds with our own rational mind and there can be conflict. But that problem can be multiplied when we have to convince friends and colleagues of our ideas, including those with the best credentials to criticise. Dr Robert Jarvik, inventor of the Jarvik-7 artificial heart, recalls how his intuition came into play when he was working on a power system for his artificial heart which used a miniature pump that had to perform in forward and reverse rotation. He and an engineer developed a computer model to work with the power system. When Dr Jarvik asked the engineer to use the model to check a certain type of design approach, the computer predicted that the performance would be miserable. 'I just knew that wasn't right', says Dr Jarvik. 'I said "I know intuitively that it will work, so build it".' The engineer reluctantly built the new model. 'It worked better than any of the systems we had built before', noted the doctor. And the engineer? He was angry. He had worked for months on the previous computer models and couldn't see their limitations. Creative thinking disturbs entrenched mindsets, so it often gets these sorts of reactions. But conflict is common in all human change and the creative person needs to have the resilience and courage to cope with this.

MIND OVER MEDICINE

The history of medicine has its own share of eureka moments, such as the discovery of penicillin which I refer to again in a later chapter. Sometimes creativity involves a process or method rather than a product — what about diagnosis, for example? A survey of radiologists reveals that the best diagnoses are not based on linear techniques, and that doctors ignore the established, sequential procedures they were taught in college and have themselves taught. Instead, each doctor has a completely different scanning technique. Asked how they arrive at their conclusions, they usually have no idea. Over time students tend to abandon the standard four-step scanning procedure and develop their own intuitive methods. One expert who likes to read EEG (electroencephalogram) wave output reports in the privacy of his own garden gives us some clues: 'I like to take an EEG, look at it rapidly the first time and form a general impression of style and character. Then I analyse it. New EEG readers are laborious, slow and conscious. As they become more experienced, it becomes a faster, *unconscious* process'. (My emphasis.)

Staying in the medical world, one surgeon, who has developed his own method of working intuitively, says that meditating helps him set up the procedure he plans to use before he sets foot in the hospital: 'The night before an operation I review it in my mind's eye and visually project what I will need to do. When I go into the operating room the next day, it's just my eyes and my hands. My rational mind is somewhere else and I operate intuitively, having prepared the night before.' This description is remarkable in a field we normally associate with highly conscious, deliberate skills of life importance.

The anti-polio vaccine

Dr Jonas Salk, who discovered the anti-polio vaccine that bears his name, wrote:

Somebody said something that seemed paradoxical to me — two things that were said did not fit together. They had to do with whether or not you had to experience infection in order to develop immunity to a virus disease. I put that in the back of my mind. Then in 1939 I found myself in a laboratory that was working on influenza. So that idea came back to me, and there was an opportunity to test it. I asked nature the question 'Is it or is it not true that you must first be infected to become immune?' And nature said ' Go ahead and design the right experiment.' I designed a series of experiments and the answer came back, 'Yes, it's possible to become immune without being infected'. You see, the answer pre-exists. What people think of as the moment of discovery is really the discovery of the question.

Salk went through similar imaginative experiences to Einstein. Early in his career, he imagined himself as an immune system and then asked what would he do to combat a virus or cancer cell. On the basis of those early conversations with himself, he began constructing hundreds of tedious laboratory experiments to come up with the answers — including those that eventually yielded his vaccine. 'But long before that', says Salk, 'this internal dialogue became second nature to me. I found my mind worked this way all the time. Others may not be conscious that they conduct this kind of dialogue, but they do. Why should it only happen to me?'

Sometimes we associate these eurekas with a single memorable breakthrough, but Salk, like many another so-called rational scientist, developed a day-to-day creativity that was an essential part of his success. He says, 'It is always with excitement that I wake up in the morning wondering what my intuition will toss up to me, like gifts from the sea. I work with it and rely on it. It's my partner.' Again, although he seems to have a 'method', it seems to be more intuitive than logical.

WINNING INTUITIVELY IN BUSINESS

Entrepreneurs have traditionally used intuitive methods, speaking of gut feelings, hunches, seat of the pants decisions, and the like. Donald Trump, in his autobiography *Trump: The Art of the Deal*, describes how he investigates properties that he plans to buy by talking to residents of the area, especially cab drivers, until he gets a gut feeling. Only then does he decide whether to proceed with the deal.

More unusually, a major investment consulting group specialises in providing clients with market advice on what they term 'disciplined intuition', which includes having a feel for a decision as well as doing proper analysis. This company is aware of the right brain/left brain significance, and talks of taking in a quantity of information through the left neocortex and allowing 'the juices of the right half' to synthesise it. Using these methods they spotted the trend in the US away from recreational jogging to walking back in 1985, a trend that was not detected by the usual research and analytical techniques. Although the mute, non-verbal right brain (like the left hand it controls) has had a bad press for centuries, it clearly accounts for amazing sophistication of thought, however alien and incomprehensible its processes seem to be.

The feel of the deal

It can apply in negotiating situations. One businessman described how, in a major negotiation, he should settle for a certain figure because, in light of all the circumstances, it 'felt right'. Bearing in mind the time and effort often involved in squeezing the last penny out of a negotiation, such as in the case of a legal claim, an intuitive decision might well turn out to be the best in the long run, even though it cannot be supported by facts and figures at the time.

Even major business acquisitions, whatever the data gathering and analysis, usually hinge on the intuitive judgement of the chief executive or a single senior person. And the decision does not necessarily go along with expensive professional advice. One business chief described the occasion when he bought a hotel on a Sunday, having viewed it on the Friday before. It was memorable to him because that purchase became the turning point in the later remarkable growth of the company. And nor was it the exception, but it seems that a lot of successful deals are traced to strong intuition and the rightness of the decision only becomes clear later when more information comes to light.

These intuitive business decisions share many of the characteristics of historical scientific and medical advances. The insight often comes when the person's mind is occupied on something else — perhaps when travelling or otherwise away from work — and has the element of pleasant surprise. He or she usually knows they have made the right decision, despite the absence of any logical basis to justify it and the intelligent criticism of knowledgeable colleagues.

Continuous creativity

Research I carried out involving top business leaders showed how important intuitive thinking is in their day-to-day work, and how, time and time again, this resulted in not just their own personal success but in the financial performance of the companies they ran. Depending often on the job role of the person involved, whether chairman or production worker, the results of creative ideas might have operational or strategic impact on the businesses.

Mark Warland of Irving Aerospace described a creative breakthrough in an earlier job concerning sticky labels in a production process. As well as the solution to this literally sticky problem being ridiculously simple in hindsight, it came from a line worker rather than the boss. This is typical of the way creative thinking can revolutionise production processes, as has happened when employees are given greater freedom to suggest and implement changes.

Don Bennett, head of Texaco UK, successfully persuaded his group management to embark on a radical approach to risk management in a massive North Sea oil exploration investment. His breakthrough came when he saw a virtual imaging video in the normal course of his work and knew instantly that this was the medium that would get his complex message across, and secure the positive decision on which the project depended. As is so often the case, that single, seemingly innocuous eureka resulted in both long term strategic changes and bottom line profits.

Grahame Winter, the boss of the Maples furnishing retailers, would travel to the USA and wander round stores, watching and listening, and return to his business more often than not with a list of ideas for implementation. In his case, he had adapted his lifestyle to accommodate his innate creativity.

Keith Oates, deputy chairman of Marks and Spencer, is similarly a gatherer of ideas and takes many overseas trips just for the purpose. Many of his ideas come intuitively and many have resulted in the successes of that company. Among other things, Keith was the architect of M&S's highly profitable diversification into financial services.

Stanley Kalms, chairman of the Dixon's retail group, who I said earlier might get half a dozen ideas before arriving at work in the morning, has also seen his spontaneous creativity translate into hard business results.

Sadly, such thinking skills do not figure in management textbooks and business school curricula, so aspiring leaders remain firmly left brain dominant and too blinkered for top management roles.

LIFE AND DEATH INSIGHTS

Examples of intuitive insights abound in every walk of life. In some cases they are of little consequence, such as when you instantly remember where you left the car keys or that you didn't let the cat out. But some result in big changes at a personal or business level. Some of the business examples I learnt of might well have affected the survival of the company and the fortunes of thousands of employees. In other cases insights may be of life and death importance.

Policemen and women and criminal investigators, for instance, tell of the importance of their 'sixth' sense in dangerous, life threatening situations, or when needing to know whether to trust an individual based on the flimsiest, brief experience. This is a similar phenomenon to powerful 'first impressions', which professional recruiters, top salespeople and gifted leaders are known to value. Similarly, accounts from armed forces personnel place a high value on the intuitive voice, which seems to have a special survival role as well as being the source of excellence in so many spheres. Usually the accounts defy rational explanation, except with the benefit of hindsight.

3

TWO-SIDED THINKING

The stories in the previous chapter confirm the importance of creative thinking for society as a whole and for us as individuals. These examples are also rich in clues as to how you and I can be more receptive to intuitive, creative thoughts. Chapter 4 addresses the common characteristics of these unconscious thinking processes and shows how you can stimulate and harness them. You will learn specific techniques to improve your performance and enjoy more or less continuous creativity. But first, a lot of the mystique can be removed by understanding how your brain processes different kinds of thoughts. Here we are especially interested in the spontaneous, unconscious kinds, examples of which we have found in science and other fields of human activity.

Any study involving the human brain, however, can do little more than scratch the surface of what is the most awesome, fantastically complex example of human life. Some scientists see the brain or human mind as the last uncharted frontier of knowledge. Some insist that, by its very nature, it is beyond our understanding. It is certainly true that the deeper we probe into its mysteries the more staggering in capacity and complexity it turns out to be. Having said this, even though so much is unknown, recent developments in neuroscience and brain scanning technology have given us an understanding of the processes way beyond anything that was known just a couple of decades ago.

Fortunately, for our present purposes, we do not need to understand how things work, let alone why we think in the way we do. Rather, we need to have some inkling of what our unique little human powerhouse can accomplish for us personally — what it can *do*. Just as important — and this is one of the secrets of great creative thinkers — we need to learn to trust it when we cannot consciously instruct it or even begin to understand its workings.

In this chapter I will describe how the two sides of the brain operate very differently and the characteristics of the different kind of thinking each is associated with. As you read on, try to match what you learn — or are reminded of — with the anecdotes you read in Chapter 2 and your own personal experience of similar occurrences.

SUPER SWITCHBOARD OR BUBBLING CAULDRON?

The brain used to be likened to a giant telephone switchboard and more recently to a digital computer. But these are poor analogies. As well as electrical impulses much chemical action is involved and in some senses the brain is more like a bubbling cauldron of chemicals than a neat and precise bit of electrical circuitry. If anything, the 'static' analogies have hindered rather than helped research. The human brain is an exhibition of electro-chemical wizardry we can only make guesses about. Nevertheless we can make simple comparisons with the hardware and software we are familiar with in the world of computers. The hardware is the physical lump of brain cells. The software is what we do with it — in other words, the programs we run that result in behaviour and achievement.

Standard issue brain

Brain hardware is fairly standard. Einstein's, for example, was average. You don't have to have a big brain or a special one to be super creative, or indeed to be intelligent or have a high IQ. However incomplete their knowledge, most experts agree on one thing; that, to all intents and purposes, the capacity of the human brain is unlimited. You don't need to change yours for a bigger central processing unit chip. The potential number of synaptic connections, or electro-chemical 'firings', is so far beyond our comprehension that the number of noughts is of academic interest only. If it is true, as many scientists assert, that we just use a small proportion of our brain capacity in any case, then the message is simple: you and I need not worry about having sufficient brain power to enjoy the sort of creative experiences I have been describing. You can trust it to do a lot more than it has done to date.

It is true, of course, that our brain cells are dying all the time. But it is also true that the more you use your brain, even in old age, the more neural or synaptic connections are made, and that is what we mean by thinking or mindpower. Your thinking capacity can increase to any level necessary just by using it. This book shows you how to use it in the areas in which it may have been underused. Thus the hardware is not the critical factor, but the software. The secret of top performance is in how you use your brain.

The genetics lottery

This is good news for the ordinary person who does not see him or herself as brainy or particularly creative. For one thing it eliminates the nagging doubt as to whether we have been genetically short-changed. Whatever part the genetics lottery might play it is completely outweighed by what you can consciously and easily do to use your brain as you want to. If we just use a tiny part of our brain capacity in the first place, any 'nature or nurture' questions — however interesting — simply do not affect our present mental capacity. You can think what you want to think, and think as much as you like, and you will not run out of brainpower. So, while we might be tempted to dismiss examples of famous or specially creative people because they are somehow special, it is encouraging to know that every one of us has more or less infinite thinking power just by virtue of being an ordinary human being. So you can affect, not just your conscious thinking, but also the unconscious processes that account for the lion's share of human achievement. The only limit is what you dare to imagine and the trust you place in your imaginings.

THINKING TWINS

Let's take a look at the average brain. The upper brain or cortex is divided physically into two parts — left and right (left is *your* left, above your left hand). Although each side, or hemisphere, is more or less identical, each operates in entirely different ways, rather like different computer operating systems that can run on the same hardware or like identical twins of very different personality. For most people, the left side is concerned with processing logical, sequential, conscious thoughts — what we usually think of as 'thinking'. Its forte is language, maths and solving problems in a step-by-step rational way.

The right side of the brain, on the other hand, is better suited to feelings, images, spatial awareness and intuition — including the sort of flashes of insight we have already seen examples of. This side of the brain is a functional hotbed of artistic, musical, scientific and common or garden everyday creativity. Conversely, there may be a rigour or form to art and music that may demand left brain processing. At the same time, as we have already seen, so-called scientific method seems to depend on eureka-type ideas. So the functional split is not as obvious as it seems at first sight.

But this functional distinction may be misleading. These specialisations are not so much to do with what the brain does (say language, maths or music) but how it does it. The right brain, for instance, treats things holistically or as a whole and happily handles issues in parallel, whereas the left brain tends to break problems into constituent parts and handles things one logical step at a time. The logic of language and maths is better suited, of course, to such linear processing. The total, holistic experience involved in art and music is better suited to right brain processing — 'It just felt right'.

Each side of your brain does what it thinks it does best, although sometimes it gets it wrong. The critical, logical, 'know-it-all' left brain, for instance, can soon suppress the ideas and natural skills of the mute, childlike right brain. Similarly, a strong feeling or half-cock idea may become action before common sense has had time to prevail. Not only can we learn to use more of each side of our brain, especially the creative right side, but we can actually choose to some extent which side to use to do the processing. Chapter 7 shows you how to get into the right 'frame of mind' to suit your particular outcome, and Chapter 8 helps you reframe any situation and to engage your right brain for creative ideas.

Convergent and divergent thinking

These different ways of processing are also termed convergent (left brain) and divergent (right brain) thinking. Convergent thinking tends to converge on a single, correct solution, as when solving a puzzle with a known answer. Divergent thinking opens up possibilities and does not accept the first convenient solution, but is ready to diverge into any direction for a better answer. Divergent, or right brain thinking, is also termed lateral or sideways thinking, as compared with left brain vertical thinking. The other main distinction of the two hemispheres is that the left side is associated with conscious thought, whereas the right side is more associated with unconscious thought or the kind of 'thought' that we cannot always control, such as feelings. We might call this kind of thinking our state of mind, which we know has a big effect on all our performance.

The left brain vehicle to our consciousness is, of course, language. Through words and other symbols, such as numbers, we can express and analyse ideas and concepts. It is difficult to imagine conscious thought without the use of language or some other symbolism. On the other hand it is hard to imagine a world without dreams, daydreams and mental images, and the pleasure of letting the mind wander from the real world around.

These different ways of thinking are familiar to us all, so it is not hard to guess at which side of the brain we will tend to use for different kinds of thinking such as spelling or multiplying, or dreaming about a new car or holiday. It is far less common to use this knowledge to develop thinking skills to positively increase our performance — to optimise externally what our brains naturally can do internally. Peak performance is about using more of your mind, training it and using it in a better way. It starts with knowing both sides of your mind, then trusting and acting upon the inarticulate unconscious side that produces the pearls of insight and creativity.

THREE BRAINS IN ONE

The brain function can be further split in a vertical way. That is, (1) the lower brain stem or reptilian brain, (2) the mid-brain or limbic system and (3) the upper brain, which is the cortex we have been discussing so far, with its two hemispheres. Certain 'hardwired' body functions such as breathing rate and blood pressure, as well as some basic human instincts such as a sense of danger and rhythm, are run from the lower, reptilian or primal brain. The mid-brain limbic system is the most chemically active and is the site of origin for our emotions. The upper brain, as we have seen, carries out reasoning and deduction (left), but it also makes associations, works in images and can 'know' intuitively (right). Here we are most concerned with the neocortex or upper brain, although right brain feelings associated with an intuition or decision ('I just felt it was right') may originate in the limbic system.

The lower brain reacts in milliseconds and well before the rational upper brain cuts in, producing feelings of anger or fear, or strong motivation that may have no rational basis, but none the less affects our every action. By its very nature, all this happens unconsciously — too quick for the conscious mind or maybe too clever in the sense that it shortcuts linear reasoning. It's a great survival mechanism when you have to outrun a grizzly bear but you can soon mess up your behaviour when handling complex modern life situations, especially when people are involved. But you don't have to act out a feeling, however strong it is, any more than you have to act on a conscious, rational decision. So this is where self-knowledge is important, including getting to know your feelings and what they mean in behaviour. You don't have to be a slave to your reptilian or limbic brains. Emotion can be positively channelled into achieving super performance rather than wasted because there is no real grizzly bear.

THINKING STAGES

Where do the eurekas and flow fit into all this? It will help to compare these models of the brain with a typical thought process, such as solving a problem or having to make a decision. In fact there are stages and these form a cycle:

➤ **Preparation** is concerned with setting a goal or defining a problem, gathering the facts and making assumptions.

➤ **Analysis** looks for patterns, tries out ideas and questions assumptions.

➤ **Frustration** occurs when we are unable to resolve a problem by conscious thought, however hard we try.

➤ **Incubation** is when we give up trying, put the matter on hold and hand it over to the unconscious mind.

➤ **Insight** is the inspiration or 'aha' moment we usually associate with creativity.

➤ **Working out** involves testing and evaluating the insights and implementing any solution.

The frustration stage is often left out, as managers and academics do not accept it happens. It should not happen, so it does not exist. In fact it is a positive help to thinking, just as pain can be for our well-being. It forces us to consciously 'drop' the problem and hand it over to our unconscious mind. The last stage is also sometimes left out, as this concerns what we do with creative ideas, rather than the creative process itself. But I am happier to define creativity as creating real things — not just ideas — which in business we normally understand by innovation. You don't stop being creative the moment you have to implement your idea. You need ongoing creativity to get round new problems you will meet.

In a formal problem-solving process these stages can usually be recognised easily, even though their timing may differ dramatically. They may well be formalised into a system to help an organisation run a project or come to an important decision. But corporations don't get frustrated; and nor, for that matter, do they get ideas — people do. And whatever systems and external structures we employ to help the thinking process, peak performance comes down to individual, subjective, right brain thinking which has no counterpart in the left brain world of the organisation.

Nor is the human system as neat as a company structure or system is, or appears to be, at least on paper. One stage may overlap into another. For example, an insight might occur during the preparation stage, having the effect of clarifying the problem or restating a question, or creatively deciding on the pertinent data required or appropriate assumptions. The final implementation stage may also present its own problems, each requiring further problem definition, periods of incubation and new insights. The incubation stage might last a few minutes, months or even years before the insight happens.

Bicameral thinking

These stages are usually stereotyped into vertical and lateral, convergent and divergent. For instance, preparation, analysis and implementation are usually considered left brain processes, whereas incubation and insight belong to the right side. In reality each stage or aspect of the thought process involves both sides of the brain, although in different degrees, which, it turns out, is what quality thinking is all about. Although a lot of conscious, left brain pondering is involved in the preparation stage, the odd inspiration might help you with creative ways to tackle the issues. Similarly, analysis may involve heavily conscious, left brain work and the danger is that we do not see the wood for the trees, being absorbed by parts rather than seeing the whole. During this stage the mind can wander, or briefly incubate a matter, drawing on right brain processing skills. Insights can improve the quality of the analysis or determine its direction. Incubation, by its very nature, happens outside consciousness, although you can consciously start the process by thinking about something completely different or just putting the problem out of your mind. Similarly, the moment of inspiration, which you cannot set a time on, is a classical creative, right brain function, although in fact this is the moment at which the insight is 'handed over' to your conscious mind. The 'aha' is the moment of consciousness. In every case both sides of your brain work hand-in-hand for quality thinking. This is bicameral or two-sided thinking and is the basis of peak performance.

So again, in these thinking stages, a brain partnership is in play, even though the processing in each brain takes place in very different ways. The eureka experiences we saw in Chapter

2 are, of course, examples of the inspiration stage. This stage may also signal the beginning of a period of high mental and physical output which we associate with flow — the very opposite of the frustration or trying harder stage. This flow experience might well see the problem through to its completion, fully implemented, as in the cases we looked at where a report or chapter of a book seemed to write itself. In other cases you may have to knuckle down and consciously work out how you will implement your ideas.

The state of flow may also be associated with a physical skill or activity, as in the case of a sport. In this case the flow is more physical than mental, but in each case it happens without conscious interference or trying and the brain is still the master controller. And even when flow seems to be entirely physical, in practice it is at such times that a person seems to display ingenuity or even genius. Thus, when playing 'in the zone', not only will a basketball player execute perfect passes and drop shots, but will somehow be able to make tactical or strategic decisions with greater clarity and insight, outsmarting the opposition. In the same way a soccer player who adds what may be termed 'imagination' to his technical skill will soon shine out as a better performer. In every case a super partnership is at work. The whole brain is marshalled to choreograph peak performance.

The secret of excellence, therefore, is not in which side of the brain is used, but in allowing either side to do what it does best. In the case of the mute right brain this means allowing it to operate without conscious interference or criticism. From the list of thinking stages it is apparent that there is a time to think consciously about a problem or goal and there is a time to stop thinking about it and hand it over to the unconscious mind. Harnessing this dual brain synergy means optimal performance.

Left brain dominance

As it happens, in modern society we tend to use the left brain much more than the right. This is so much the case that in many people the imaginative, creative right brain is all but atrophied, just like a muscle that has not been used for a long time. Ideally you just need to allow your brain to do its own thing. In reality, however, there may be such an imbalance that you have to stimulate right brain thinking to ensure that your creative skills are given a chance. As we have seen, a simple way is to put a problem out of your mind in order to incubate it, just by thinking about or doing something else. You can also use techniques such as brainstorming and other more recently developed methods to help stir the creative juices (Chapter 8). Or it may require a change of attitude or lifestyle and Chapter 7 shows you how you can make these changes. The result of all this will be more and better insights or eurekas, and more frequent and extended periods of peak flow performance.

THE THINKING SPECTRUM

Another important distinction is between conscious and unconscious thinking. At one extreme we can be very aware and focused, and at the other extreme preoccupied with inner thoughts, daydreaming or indeed dreaming. In between are the different states of mind we are all very familiar with, such as when we are only partly tuned into a conversation or what is going on around. At one moment you may be aware of what is happening around you or consciously addressing a problem and at the next moment musing on some inner thought, imagining a scenario miles away, or in the past or future. You may 'discuss' things internally — talking to yourself — or access images and feelings, oblivious, for the moment, of the world around you. Or you may simply let your mind wander on to some aspect of the matter, as a bee flits from flower to flower. Thus our thinking swings continuously along a spectrum of highly conscious to unconscious, external to internal, focused to preoccupied, left brain to right brain.

Both sides of your brain are operating all the time, say in addressing an issue, solving a problem or simply living in and relating to the outside world. But in terms of conscious thought you are either conscious or not conscious of your external world, or somewhere in between. You will tend either to focus outward or inward. On the one hand you will use your senses to represent 'real' things, people and events around you, and on the other hand you will use your inner senses (seeing images, hearing sounds, experiencing feelings), quite oblivious, during that time, of external reality. For example, you may drive several miles, not remembering anything about the journey at all, because your mind has been on other things. During all that time your reality is an inner reality — you may have been thinking about your children, a forthcoming holiday, facing an important meeting at work or whatever. Then there are times when we hover between the two extremes, such as when taking part in a conversation while listening to music or, reverting to the driving example, partly aware of the traffic conditions, but with half an ear on the car radio and the other half engaged in casual conversation with a passenger. During waking hours, and right through our thinking lives, we move continuously up and down the thinking spectrum.

Uptime and downtime

The high focus end of the spectrum is termed uptime and the bottom end — with the extreme of dreaming — is termed downtime. Using this analogy, of a *range* of consciousness if you like, or thinking spectrum, you can move positively towards uptime or downtime, depending on your personal tendency and your present need to be more creative or more focused and organised. You can start to take control and *manage* your thinking spectrum. A person who is forever daydreaming, losing attention and maybe missing important appointments, for instance, should consider spending more time in uptime. The message for you is 'Be more focused, more aware, pay attention to what is actually going on around you. Simply watch, listen and feel.'

It is far more common, however, especially at work and in management, to be too externally focused, and not give enough time for intuition and imagination to flourish, or to incubate our thoughts. This is the equivalent of left brain dominance. In this case the answer is to spend more time in downtime, let your mind wander and get inside your inner world more often. Relax and develop your personal 'space'. Don't try too hard for too long. Switch your mind to something else. This is the thinking mode where the eurekas and flow happen, where you are more likely to be creative and where peak performance tends to be reached.

We don't get taught at school about how we think and people who think about thinking tend to do it by default rather than by design, and often later in life. But there is no doubt that understanding how you think personally is an invaluable aspect of self-knowledge and self-development. Some people have a tendency to grind away at a problem long after they have stopped moving towards a solution — spinning the wheels, getting frustrated and wasting time. Others will quickly sense when they are coming to a mental impasse and will switch to another activity, 'sleeping' on their problem. In most cases a solution will present itself by the following day or maybe during the night. With experience, they learn to manage their thinking spectrum.

There is a lot to be gained from this form of self-management. Apart from dominant uptime being hard on your health because of the stress it causes, it is an inefficient, unbalanced use of the brain. Simply knowing this solves half the problem. Sometimes we only have to discover our latent right brain which has been there all the time. Shedding a macho tendency to always make instant decisions or never to let a matter drop until we have solved it, to be always in control, may be another area for unlearning. For some this will mean a complete change of attitude and maybe even lifestyle. But we can all acquire the skill of moving at will up and down the thinking spectrum in a way that makes the best use of our bicameral thinking resources. In

Chapter 7 you will learn how to get into the right relaxed frame of mind, perhaps by a change of lifestyle rather than techniques. In Chapter 8 you will learn specific techniques to move along your uptime downtime thinking spectrum for specific purposes — such as to achieve a goal or solve a problem — and so release all your latent creative powers for peak performance.

We have seen four major aspects of the brain and how we think:

➤ The **two hemispheres** and what is termed hemispherical polarisation give us a lot of information about how thoughts are processed — at one side logically and sequentially, and at the other side holistically or in parallel.

➤ The **three-part brain** which involves primitive feelings and reactions as well as the rational thinking we usually associate with *Homo sapiens*.

➤ The **stages** in the typical thinking process, throughout which both left and right brain elements work in close partnership and accomplish very different but complementary activities.

➤ The **thinking spectrum** and the role of the unconscious mind.

So the black hole of the unconscious mind starts to make sense in how it affects everything we do. Information is power and self-knowledge can mean power over your mind-body, and control over how you use it to achieve top performance. To operate at peak performance you cannot run on two cylinders. You have to put your whole mind to what you are doing, then let your whole mind *put you* to doing what is best to achieve the outcomes you have set.

4

LIFE-CHANGING LESSONS IN CREATIVITY

Y ou have now seen some of the ways your mind does the clever things it does, even things we sometimes don't appreciate. The examples in Chapter 2 showed us how important creative thinking is to all performance and how ideas are transformed into innovations that meet needs and affect lives and whole societies. In the first part of this chapter I will draw out some simple principles from the examples we met in Chapter 2 and what we learnt about the brain in Chapter 3. In the second part I will suggest some situations in which you can apply the lessons and start to see benefits.

FROM ORDINARY TO EXTRAORDINARY

From what we have learnt about our brain we can be certain that the intuitive 'gift' is not just for a chosen few. It is universal, applying to any person and any sort of activity. For example, it has been established that there is no correlation between high intelligence and creativity. It is the case that creative people tend to be of above average intelligence (as measured by IQ), but it is not the case that people with a high IQ tend to be particularly creative or for that matter that they turn out to be achievers in any other sense. Some of the inventors and artists we met in Chapter 2 might not have scored well on an IQ test. Many, like some of today's top achievers such as Microsoft CEO Bill Gates, would not even have finished their college education.

Innovations tend to come, not from the mainstream of a science, profession or industry, but from the fringe, or in many cases from a completely different industry or field of knowledge. Again, ordinary people, rather than the experts you would expect, get the breakthrough ideas. Even musicians and artists of genius do not take personal credit for their gifts, and often attribute their creativity to an outer source. Sometimes naïve questions rather than clever answers are the key to the biggest breakthroughs and experts are not prone to ask naïve questions. With hindsight, most solutions turn out to be simple or just common sense. 'Why didn't I think of that?' or 'It's so obvious' are typical responses to great ideas. So the first lesson both from history and neurophysiology is that we can all achieve much more with our standard brain resource.

Nevertheless we do tend to associate great creative thinking with names like Einstein, Archimedes or famous entrepreneurs of our day. In most cases, however, the fame seems to have followed the childlike creative thinking, rather than there being some special qualification or ability needed to be creative. For instance, Archimedes is probably remembered more for his 'Eureka!' exclamation and jumping out of his bathtub than for any of his real achievements, let alone the scientific principle of displacement. And Elias Howe is remembered not so much for inventing the sewing machine as by the way it happened in a strange dream involving spear-wielding natives. If he had worked it out logically or conducted a market survey he might not be remembered today. Apart from having a funny dream he was as ordinary as anybody else.

When it comes to creativity, flashes of inspiration and all the thinking power of the imaginative right brain, the rule is simple, and it's a lesson worth learning: 'If anyone can, I can'. Zen said something even more significant for peak performance: 'If you can do anything well, you can do everything well'.

There is no super club for the specially gifted. Check out the diverse backgrounds and formal qualifications of the examples I gave in Chapter 2. If creativity is a gift, then the gift is the ability we all have to use our fantastic brain resource in a natural way. So, rather than just admiring or envying those who seem to be naturally creative and seem to achieve anything with ease and flair, we can learn from them, as well as from our own more creative experiences. Life-changing lessons are there for the learning, by ordinary people.

LESSONS TO UNLEARN

A different kind of learning is needed, however. Learning to be creative or to use your imagination does not come about by technical training or indeed any logical, left brain three-step or ten-step process. You can't learn, for instance, how to call up a eureka by lunchtime or to receive the answer to a particular problem you have on demand. Nor can you guarantee that today you will sail through all your work with ease and inspiration without setbacks, frustration and hard work, as maybe you have done on previous occasions. The process is more to do with unlearning, and regaining the imagination, sensitivity and trust you had as a child. This may involve beliefs, attitudes and lifestyle, which I cover in Chapter 7. Having recaptured your childlike, creative imagination you can draw on a far larger adult experience base and apply your new thinking to bigger issues. For the moment, unlearning just means having an open mind.

As well as unlearning, there are also positive things you can do. For instance, you can be more ready to accept insights when they do come and thus get far more out of them. How many times have you quickly put an idea out of your mind because it was a bit far-fetched or you would have a job convincing so-and-so in the finance department? As we have seen, imagination turns into behaviour and ideas can become innovations. You can start to trust even the flimsiest of intuitive feelings.

This takes practice, especially if you have been in the habit of suppressing your ideas or of self-criticism. But you can make a start by following the simple principles in this chapter. Then by making a few changes in lifestyle, as we shall see in Chapter 7, you can increase the number of intuitive insights you get, even though you cannot tie them down to time and place. Applying the principles and techniques you will learn you can even increase the quality, or usefulness, as well as quantity, of your right brain ideas. And you can make those precious times of flow, or being 'in the groove', far more frequent than they have been hitherto, as well as directing them to specific areas of your life that they have not been associated with before. So the two phenomena which account for the extraordinary success of top achievers are within your control. You determine the pace and level of your performance in any area. Only you can achieve your best.

Most of this training involves just a few commonsense principles, in addition to an appreciation of the way the brain works, and the thinking stages, as we saw in the previous chapter. This is the simple but vital foundation you will need before you start using the techniques I describe in Chapters 7 and 8. Adopting new mindsets means abandoning others — that's the unlearning.

TRAINING PRINCIPLES

Here are some important principles, drawn from the examples in Chapters 2 and what we learnt in Chapter 3 about the mind, that will help you to be more creative and achieve more of the things you want. Apply them first mentally — check them out for common sense and imagine the circumstances in which they could be applied. Then apply them practically, committing yourself to the actions suggested.

Ideas don't come in a vacuum

However extraordinary or mysterious the historical examples of 'eurekas' seem to be, with hindsight they usually turn out to be both simple and logical — the sort of idea that anyone could have come up with, given a reasonable knowledge of the subject in question. More particularly, they are not useless, dreamlike bits of information but answers to specific needs and problems, or they help you to achieve your specific goals and purposes — even those you may not have expressed. We are all goal-achieving mechanisms and we don't work well without goals. Intuition has a purpose.

Take the simple case of remembering a person's name from years ago. You have usually already been giving it thought ('What's her name again?') or at least thinking about something related to the person. The name recollection had a purpose. So the revelation, although not earth-shattering, when it comes, means something. Similarly, if you receive a few good ideas in the shower first thing in the morning the chances are these will relate to work or personal issues that you have been concerned with either before you went to sleep, or in the days or weeks before. Moreover, if you act on them, the chances are you will get benefit by fulfilling your objectives or solving problems — they will be useful. Whatever you are involved in, creative ideas can dramatically improve your performance.

The link between insight and outcome is not always obvious and direct, however. But if your main preoccupation is with your health, then it is not surprising that your good ideas tend to be about your health, even if not addressing a specific 'problem'. Similarly, if you are concerned about ways to make money, it will follow that you will get ideas, however bizarre or surprising they are, that will help you achieve your outcome of making money. Your goals or personal 'agenda' will determine the kind of insights you receive, however random they may seem.

You may not always be conscious of underlying desires, but your unconscious mind will nevertheless take them into consideration. Thus some insights, although interesting and surprising, may not easily fit into a known problem or issue you are currently aware of. You might ask 'Why on earth did I think of that?' Often the value of an insight emerges much later. Either way, ideas don't happen in a vacuum but something triggers them: a goal, a problem, a need, a wish, a dream. They are aligned to your purposes. In the examples given in Chapter 2:

➤ It was when Dr Jonas Salk was working on influenza that the idea (about infection and immunity) came to him. The idea addressed precisely what he was most concerned about at the time.

➤ James Watson and Francis Crick had worked intensively on DNA structure before the double helix revelation came. The insight was crucial to their main purpose.

➤ The mathematician Poincaré laboured for fifteen days trying 'a great number of combinations' before his Fuchscian function breakthrough. There was little doubt what was on his mind or at least in the back of his mind.

➤ Inventor Art Fry started with a real problem — bookmarks which fell from his hymnal in the choir — which his Post-It notes solved. Further outcomes (to make money, become famous or whatever) were later fulfilled as the idea was exploited and no doubt new insights received.

➤ Elias Howe had worked for years on his prototype sewing machine before his remarkable dream gave him the breakthrough.

➤ The musician's aims may have been no more specific than to create beautiful music or to fulfil a patron's commission; but that was enough for the subconscious, creative mind to go to work on.

Each 'I found it' (eureka) found something that was being

searched for. Each right brain revelation was for a purpose. Ideas made sense in the light of a need or preoccupation. The human brain, although infinite in its capacity and richness, is economic and goal oriented in its operation.

Wishes and wants

This principle applies to whatever is important to you in the sense that it occupies a large part of your waking life, such as your job, a big domestic issue or a hobby you are captivated with. It works by association. If you buy a new outfit and wear it for a party you will soon notice if someone else is wearing the same outfit. Before you bought it it had no meaning to you, so no association was made. Similarly, if you change your car, suddenly that model seems to be everywhere on the roads. You associate otherwise meaningless bits of information or experience because they have meaning to you. Ideas pop 'to the surface' when something of the millions of sensory stimuli you receive moment by moment associates with an existing meaning, need or purpose. Your unspoken wishes are the constant command of your ever-alert subconscious brain, which combs new and existing data to help your dreams become reality.

The principle applies equally to specific goals or outcomes that you have clearly and consciously set in your mind, even if you have not decided how they will be achieved and they have not yet become problems. In practice, of course, not every wish or goal results in flashes of inspiration about how you can achieve it, let alone materialises as eventual reality. Consequently many wishes remain unrealised. Your goal may need to be more than just a wish or even a written statement of your objectives. For the creative right brain to click into gear there is usually the need for a more sensory representation of what you want. So your goal has to be internalised, in the form of sights, sounds and feelings that in effect pre-experience your outcome. This inner experience then becomes the hotbed of creative insights. The more real your inner goal is, the more your whole brain will work towards achieving it. In Chapter 7 I describe a simple technique that will help you to make your goals more compelling and amenable to creative insights — in other words, how to turn wishes into wants or burning desires that your whole 'system' will act out into reality.

When to stop thinking

Another lesson from this principle is that, at some stage, you do need to think about your goals and problems consciously. The mistake is to dwell consciously on how you will achieve them. The unknown variables are too much for your conscious brain to cope with. That's where the need for trust in intuitive, moment-by-moment 'guidance' comes in. Spontaneous thoughts that come to your conscious mind in an apparently random way usually relate to your present needs and problems or matters that are important to you. They don't happen for no reason. The secret is in knowing when to stop consciously thinking, when to stop trying and when to hand over the matter to your unconscious mind. As we learnt in the Thinking Stages model (Chapter 3), you do that when you seem to be getting nowhere and frustration sets in.

Intuitions are usually in response to clearly established goals and purposes. So, in order to get them going:

➤ decide what you want;

➤ make your goals specific and preferably measurable;

➤ visualise your goals and objectives internally (see Chapter 7);

➤ have a purpose in anything you do;

➤ dream new dreams and make them real by repeatedly seeing, hearing and feeling them as being fulfilled;

➤ trust your creative mind to turn them into reality, just as a child trusts a parent to keep a promise;

➤ concentrate your mind on where you want to be, rather than on the detail of how you are going to get there;

➤ think of 10 outcomes and expect 100 ideas to help you achieve them;

➤ check out your goals against each other in case you are pulling in different directions;

➤ increase or decrease the size of your outcomes so that they are always motivating. You can usually break a goal into manageable chunks or increase a challenge by shortening the timescale for the task.

GIGO and how to generate quality ideas

What about the quality or usefulness of the ideas you get? The well-known computer rule GIGO — 'garbage in garbage out' — has its place also in creative thinking. Let me start by introducing the terms 'intuition with precedent', and 'intuition without precedent'.

Intuition with precedent

Intuition is knowing something without knowing how you know it. You don't arrive at an insight by a logical or even conscious process. Intuition with precedent draws on your experience and existing knowledge — your memory database of the world as you have experienced or perceived it. The insight 'knowledge' is not new when it comes, it just comes in a different form. Any eureka seems unique and may be surprising because of the way existing knowledge and experience has been used, or synthesised, rather than the knowledge or issues per se.

For example, you know Molly has first-class organising skills but there is no need for them in the present winding down of her section. But you hear of a project in another department for which she would be ideally suited, so both she and the company will benefit. Two problems, if you like, cancel each other out to create a better win-win outcome.

Or when trying to boost revenues on an ailing product range, you hear of a simple new application that can generate sales without new investment. In each case the insight is greater than the sum of the bits of your experience it draws upon.

In the case of Elias Howe, who invented the sewing machine, the novelty was in linking a needle on a machine for sewing to the special spear he dreamt about. The knowledge and experience (of spears and machines) were there already and were unremarkable. The clever part was the unique association that created the breakthrough synergy. Our own 'aha' revelations may not seem remarkable to other people. But it often seems to us that such reasoning would not be arrived at by logical thinking 'in a thousand years'.

Under this definition of intuition, 'there is nothing new under the sun'. You have simply seen things in a different light, reframed a situation or made unusual associations. Neurologically, you have created new neural pathways in your brain. So ideas depend on your existing 'experience base'. And this experience can be controlled, from now on. You decide on your lifestyle, whom you associate with, what you read and what your senses take in.

Intuition without precedent

Intuition without precedent, on the other hand, relates to those insights or bits of knowledge that cannot be attributed to existing experience. In other words there is no way to account for the intuition, even with the benefit of hindsight. It seems to have come from an external source or in some supernatural way. This of course is the case with many examples of extra-sensory perception (ESP). In many of the examples in Chapter 2 it seemed as though the revelation came from outside — like 'a gift from the gods', as it has been described over the ages. Dr Jonas Salk described his intuitions as 'gifts from the sea'. Richard Bach maintains that his best-selling book *Jonathan Livingston Seagull* merely came 'through him'. 'I didn't write it', he asserts. On the face of it these are examples of intuition without precedent.

But with our present knowledge of the brain's amazing ability both to store memories and make these associations it is obvious that most of these are examples of intuition with precedent. The bringing together or synthesis of bits of knowledge or experience seem like original ideas, but only the association is new — the component parts were there all the time. We have already seen how the problem or goal was already 'internalised'. New angles or combinations made all the difference.

There is more than enough evidence of the power of our creative minds in the form of intuition with precedent to account for any degree of creativity and super performance. So we need not resort to paranormal explanations, at least for the practical purpose of achieving personal excellence. In some cases your own insight may seem to be based on information outside your memory database of experience. But this may underestimate the sheer scale and richness of our lifetime experience, composed as it is of imaginings as well as reality, and of memories of memories ad infinitum. Through reading, television and travel, whole new worlds on our mental hard disks are now available for our intuition to draw upon.

Trashy ideas

Here is the significance of the GIGO principle. Because your 'with precedence' intuition draws on your database of experience, it will be affected by the quantity and quality of that experience. Thus as a person gets older, for example, he or she might become more intuitive, drawing upon more and more experience. Conversely, a young child's insights, although often fascinating, will depend more on synthesising the here and now, or his or her limited past experience. The so-called 'wisdom' of an older person, usually of an intuitive nature, reflects a wealth of such experience, in its diversity and quality, as well as its sheer quantity. Put more starkly, a person who reads trashy literature will usually have trashy ideas, of a quality that reflects what their mind is full of. In a similar way, by associating with bright, stimulating people we are more likely to come up with ideas that reflect the quality of our mental input. Quality in, quality out:

garbage in, garbage out. So you can influence the quality of your ideas by the inputs you seek and allow to enter your experience. IQ is not the issue, but perhaps there is need for a common sense adjustment of habits and lifestyle.

Broadening your mind

The GIGO principle is closely related to the more basic idea of having a wide range of interests and experiences to form the basis of your ideas. Some fascinating aspects of this principle came out in my research with chief executive officers. Contrary to the popular workaholic stereotype, those who seemed to be the most creative tended to have wide interests outside their normal business life. These interests might be in the arts, a hobby or pastime, or come about perhaps through socialising with a different class of people than would be usual in their role. The insights they received, it turned out, were usually because of the richness of this 'outside' exposure rather than their long expertise in the job or industry.

How this mind-broadening process happened varied from person to person. An introvert might be a voracious reader, for instance, whereas an extrovert might depend on talking to other people, taking an active interest in their work, ideas and experience. Holistic thinkers such as these have often had a good broad education, even if much of their expertise was self-taught. In a similar way many important inventions and scientific breakthroughs have come from people outside the mainstream of 'correct' thinking — rebels, if you like, within their field of work. All this suggests that a wide rather than very deep knowledge and experience base fosters creativity and high performance.

On this basis anyone can be more creative, because the quantity and quality of what you take in through your senses is largely within your control. You can choose your hobbies and pastimes, what you read and how much, whom you associate with, where you travel to and so on. You can determine what your personal experience 'library' or database will comprise:

gossip, unsupported opinions and banality on the one hand; or the cream of your culture, and other cultures, by way of their history, art, literature and science on the other.

The big mistake we all tend to make is to undervalue any time not spent on specific, and usually short-term, goals, whether business or personal. But the right brain has a lot to contribute in areas we have not associated with the creative mind. The less direct benefits of a richer, more relaxed way of life are not appreciated. See my book *The Right Brain Time Manager* (Piatkus, 1995) which covers the 'other side' of time management, for example, in more detail. So many enlightened business leaders I have met could trace their intuitive ideas to concrete business results, so they were more than repaid for their apparently less rigorous use of time. So be open to new ways of doing things, people, cultures and opinions. This is what creates the pool of rich experience on which the intuitive mind will draw and determines the quality of what it produces.

There is a lot you can do to apply the lessons of GIGO:

➤ Extend your hobbies and interests.

➤ Develop a richer, more varied lifestyle.

➤ Take on new experiences and challenges.

➤ Meet new people, outside your work and immediate circle of friends.

➤ See new places. Get off the beaten track.

➤ Read more, but be choosy.

➤ Expose yourself to quality experience inputs. Second-hand experiences, like television, are fine, but again be choosy.

➤ Start to trust ideas, whether with or without precedent.

➤ Don't demand chapter and verse before acting on a hunch or gut feeling.

➤ Get practice first in small things — don't sell the company or get a divorce on a fleeting gut feeling.

➤ Watch out for prejudice and wishful thinking (not based on well-formed, realistic goals).

Stop trying

In the Thinking Stages model described in Chapter 3 we saw the importance of incubation or 'sleeping on a problem'. This is hard to swallow for most intelligent people. We have been programmed to try, try and try again, to work harder, concentrate and be decisive. So it seems unnatural to put matters right out of our mind, especially if they are important and there is a timescale involved. In management, indecision is positively frowned upon, and incubation smacks of weakness, passiveness and procrastination. But right brain thinking is all to do with quality — effective thinking rather than appearances or conformity to business or other norms. It sees the whole picture, and thus gets things in perspective.

Sir Richard Greenbury, chairman of Marks and Spencer (see my book *Think Like a Leader*), makes a point of not taking important decisions late in the day, knowing that a good night's sleep often brings with it a solution or another angle on the problem. Seasoned executives know well that few decisions are so important that they cannot wait twenty-four hours. If every decision is super urgent and you spend your time firefighting, the chances are there is a bigger, more endemic problem that needs far more than macho decisiveness. Expensive crises can be avoided or forestalled — that's what good management is all about. To avoid a future crisis, creative insights and perspective, and the incubation period they usually demand, are even more important. You will need to see things beyond the obvious and the signals may be obscure. Logic cannot handle the future and there are few cases in today's world where you can safely extrapolate from the past. In some cases, of course, the problem seems to dissolve or resolve itself in the light of a new day or with the passage of time. In other cases new information comes to hand which improves the quality of the decision. For some people it may be harder to stop trying than to keep trying, they are so conditioned. It certainly takes practice and probably a change of attitude. But it is smarter to use your whole brain than just the conscious 'trying' part.

The important point is that right brain thinking can only be processed in this unconscious, apparently uncontrolled way. It is not helped by trying harder and harder. There is no other way to harness this side of your brain, which might help to explain the compulsory human fact of nightly incubation — or sleep — during which so much of this mental processing takes place. Even if you have a deadline, although you cannot guarantee a right brain insight to fit it, by unloading your conscious mind of the problem, even for half an hour, you will at least give your unconscious mind a chance to work. Paradoxically, this may actually help you to reach important deadlines by clear thinking and time-saving short-cut ideas.

People have often said that a twenty-minute walk round the local park or just switching off for a while to something entirely different is enough to clear their mind and give a fresh approach. We saw that Poincaré, the famous mathematician, was 'walking on the bluff' when his great Fuchsian function insight came. Later it was when 'walking along the street' that the solution to further problems came to him. Richard Bach was walking along the beach front when *Jonathan Livingston Seagull* was conceived. And Mozart became prolific when walking after a good meal. Whatever means you adopt, for a while you have to stop trying.

For people in sedentary jobs, it may be that physical exercise or sport is more effective than just mentally switching to other issues. At home, energetically cleaning out the cupboards or pulling up weeds in the garden might be the best way to make the mental switch. In any case, once you have given your problem reasonable thought and marshalled the facts together, you have to stop trying and start trusting.

How to stop trying and start trusting:

➤ If at first you don't succeed, try once more then pack it in.

Better still, try something *different*.

➤ Take it easy. Think about the quickest, easiest way to do what you have to do.

➤ When you become frustrated, do something else, completely different. Sleep on the problem. Trust your unconscious mind to come up with the answer when it is ready.

➤ Don't commit yourself to deadlines you might regret — in the long run you will not get credit, either in respect from others or career progress.

➤ Don't make an important decision that can be put off until tomorrow. By then the problem might have gone, new information may be available or you may have received a eureka solution.

Just relax

I started by saying that peak performance is achieved by a mind-body partnership. Physical relaxation, of course, is related to your state of mind. When you are relaxed it is much easier to switch off from pressing problems. It is the busy, 'chattering' mind that will go over a problem so many times and from so many angles that it seems to grow out of all proportion, and the answer seems to move farther away. So many examples of creative thinking happen when people are reasonably content with themselves and physically relaxed. Einstein was lying on a sun-drenched grassy hillside when he imagined he was doing a cosmic trip on a beam of light. Kekulé was in a semi-sleep state when he dreamt of the snake-like creatures chasing each other's tales that resulted in the benzene ring discovery. And the creative walks I mentioned earlier were obviously pleasant, relaxing times. In the case of business executives the most creative situations range from showering and bathing to gardening and travelling. In each case the person was away from the detail and pressure of everyday work, and was doing something that helped them to relax and get their mind off stressful matters. Of course people are able to relax in different ways and if you don't like driving or gardening then such pastimes will do little for your creativity. So do whatever helps you to relax and try the specific relaxation techniques described in Chapter 7.

Pleasure and pain

The important thing is to get into a pleasurable rather than painful state. I have found that dedicated joggers or walkers have an enormous creative outlet in that pastime, while others experience the same activities as mentally sterile. Similarly, an executive who enjoyed washing his car got a stream of ideas each Sunday morning, while a colleague might be reaping the same creative benefits from a slow hot bath, or nurturing begonias. If you squeeze these relaxing, private times out of your life, in true time management textbook fashion, you will squeeze out spontaneous ideas that could benefit you. And you will probably pile up stress-related ills into the bargain.

Not surprisingly, what is good for your mind is also good for your physical health and well-being. The medical case for a more carefree approach to life is overwhelming. Harmful stress is a killer. So make time to get away from things, however briefly, when you feel they are getting out of control, and you become tense, irritable and unproductive. Then, for the longer term, build into your life relaxing pleasurable 'thinking times' on a regular basis, so that they become daily and weekly habits. Such apparently unproductive freewheeling thinking or dreaming time is a great investment in your health and achievement. This is just a principle, of course, and has to be applied with common sense. You may have to use specific techniques that will help you to relax (Chapter 7) or start up pastimes and hobbies that will help you regularly take your mind off work and everyday problems. The benefits more than repay these simple changes in priority and lifestyle. A relaxed approach to life, however strong your desires or goals, is a key to peak performance.

Start straight away:

➤ Relax frequently. Try the exercises in Chapter 7.

➤ Take a course in relaxation techniques and practise it whenever you get a free moment.

➤ Take a few minutes off during the day to wind down.

➤ Take holidays — even short ones — especially when you feel things are crowding in on you.

➤ Use your imagination to visualise pleasant thoughts that will help you get in the right, creative frame of mind.

➤ Decide what you enjoy best and can feasibly fit into your lifestyle.

➤ Change your lifestyle to do what you want to do.

The value of a good question

Einstein wrote of 'raising new questions'. Dr Jonas Salk, intriguingly 'asked nature the question'. He also wrote, intriguingly: 'You see, the answer pre-exists. What people think of as the moment of discovery is really the discovery of the question.'

Incessant questioning is a common enough trait in small children. They are not concerned about asking stupid questions or worried about displaying a lack of knowledge. It's natural for them to ask questions about everything. Children who somehow overcome the inhibiting conditioning of their education and the adult world can go on to extraordinary accomplishments, whether in science, art, business or whatever. But few Western adults get through ubiquitous left brain conditioning to become holistic, questioning thinkers. Few achieve their potential. Very few pose questions with the sense of discovery and excitement that they did as children. Without this basic know-how, very few become peak performers.

Yet here lies one of the secrets of perpetual creativity and excellence. We are all pretty well programmed to solve problems and answer questions, whether of a practical or abstract nature. And you can soon get promotion as a manager if you can repeatedly answer the questions and solve the problems posed to you. But that does not account for peak performance — plenty of employees do well as problem-solving machines, although computers are quickly taking over their work. But the person who asks the right question stands out. That is one characteristic of a leader who quickly gets to the core of an issue. A question can change the whole nature of a so-called problem or even turn the problem into an opportunity. It can reframe, or change the perspective, so that you see things from another angle altogether. And that is the sort of right brain insight that marks excellence rather than competence.

If you're given the question, or problem, the tendency is to address its parts and analyse it in a logical, step-by-step (left brain) way. The chances are that you will get a single, reasonable, feasible answer. You will never know if it was the best answer or whether you were solving the right problem. If you are open to different questions, you are open to different and better answers — perhaps choices.

Looking for questions rather than answers can be frightening for the dyed-in-the-wool left brain thinker. You have no data, no given problem to put your mind to. You don't know where to start. You don't know how to use your brain or what to address. And this is where childlike questioning comes into play. Questions seem to come from nowhere and you certainly cannot logically account for every fleeting question that flits through your head — 'Why did I ask that?' Hence the feeling that the answer pre-exists, as do the questions that will unlock the solutions.

'A good question is 80 per cent of the way to the answer' is the way it is sometimes expressed. Put another way, one good question is worth a lot of pat, logical answers. You don't get to discover new territories by following the well-worn tracks of conventional logic. Originality and personal excellence comes from the vast untapped resource of your own life experience, and it is harnessed by the clever way your right brain searches, associates and synthesises to produce priceless insightful questions.

To ask good questions:

➤ get into a questioning mode;

➤ ask why, when, where, what, how, who;

➤ change your routines so that you notice different things;

➤ be curious;

➤ be a little adventurous;

➤ be prepared to get below the surface of what seems obvious;

➤ expect surprises;

➤ be prepared to look foolish in the case of nine questions out of ten that you ask;

➤ have clear personal goals towards which your enquiring mind can be directed.

See old problems from a new angle

Einstein wrote that 'to regard old problems from a new angle requires creative imagination, and marks real advance in science'. This is termed reframing and is the secret of the creativity that translates into peak performance. Most great innovations seem common sense with hindsight and not very remarkable. In many cases you wonder why you did not think of the idea yourself. The reason is simple; there is nothing new. You just look at things in a different way or bring together ideas and things that previously did not associate with each other. In some cases a slight change of angle is enough. In other cases conventional wisdom has to be turned on its head. Either way the result is new and surprising to you. And it has benefits, because it did not happen in a vacuum, but was addressing some goal or purpose. And it came through the painless, usually enjoyable process of reframing.

Sadly the way we think in a pattern mode, with everything in familiar mindset pigeon holes, does not lend itself to reframing. We tend to look for the quickest, most obvious meaning in anything we see, hear and feel rather than a new or different meaning. So it doesn't come naturally, at least not after years of thinking in a set way. In Chapter 7 I suggest ways you can get into the right frame of mind to see things in a different way, if need be by changing your self-belief about your creativity. Then in Chapter 8 I describe specific reframing tools you can apply in particular situations, such as when faced with a major decision or confronted with an intractable problem. But there is no step-by-step way to an insight or a new angle — you just have to start with an open mind and use the tools to stimulate your innate creativity. Applying the simple lessons in this chapter and the techniques in Chapters 7 and 8 will soon get you into the habit of thinking creatively.

To start thinking creatively:

➤ Look at things in a different way.

➤ Change some aspect of a situation — for instance what if your boss was the new office junior, what if you knew you would succeed before you started, what if you had the best people in the world advising you?

➤ Change the context — what if this happened outside of work, say in a social setting? What if it was in a different culture and country? What if it had happened fifty years ago — or will happen ten years in the future?

➤ Change some aspect of what you think you see, hear and feel. Could there be a different meaning?

➤ Change your daily and weekly routines so that you start to see things you would not have noticed before or the same things in a different light.

Get away from the crowds

Time after time creative ideas have come to people when they were on their own. Or even when in a crowd — say at an airport, in a busy hotel lounge or railway carriage — where they were anonymous and undisturbed. Insights tend to come when we are in downtime (described in Chapter 3) and this is when we are in our inner world of the senses rather than the outer world. Relating to people, however sociable you are, means staying in uptime most of the time if you are not to be rude and cause offence.

On the several occasions when Poincaré described his remarkable spontaneous ideas he was on his own — whether walking at the seaside, along a busy street in town or at least left to his own thoughts, such as when sitting on a bus. Mozart makes a special point of this, writing about 'when I am, as it were, completely myself, entirely alone'. He later writes, 'provided I am not disturbed', and this is another important feature of creative thinking. If your creative mind expects to be disturbed it will tend to clam up. Thus, even when alone in your office at work, if at any moment the door could open or the telephone ring, the subconscious mind tends to stay below the surface. It needs time and it wants your attention. Conversely, in a foreign airport, or railway train, however crowded, downtime can be very productive. In these cases it takes a little practice to be able to exclude all the distractions around you.

Interestingly, this seems to apply even in the case of extrovert people who enjoy and benefit from the company of others. Yet even when, in these cases, they may draw ideas and information in discussion with colleagues, their most creative experiences are usually when alone.

In research I did among top British businesspeople for my book *Think Like a Leader* there were one or two apparent exceptions. In one case an historic breakthrough came when a CEO was on a long flight with a close business partner, during which the ideas they bounced off each other produced a memorable breakthrough resulting in a massive project. The chances are, however, that over the long period of the flight each of them was able to engage in plenty of downtime, notwithstanding the presence of a close colleague — just as in the case of husband and wife there can be periods of silence without self-consciousness or embarrassment. Close business colleagues and friends get used to each other's 'wavelength' and in time seem to read each other's minds. Such a relationship is well fostered and can help creativity.

I found, however, that this is the exception rather than the rule. The lesson from top leaders is clear: your individual brain has the capacity to tackle almost any problem and does not depend on outside resources, including other brains. In some situations, such as group brainstorming sessions, the group dynamics actually works against creativity, as personalties, roles, 'pecking order' and company politics constrain completely free expression. The lesson from history is as overwhelming as from contemporary business: get away from it all, long enough to give your unconscious mind a bit of space and in an environment where you will not be interrupted.

You will need to work out for yourself how this lesson can be applied. For some people with full 'uptime' lives and rarely a moment to themselves it might be difficult, and require a big change in lifestyle, and I cover this further in Chapter 7. But it can usually be accommodated easily. You have probably noticed top sportspeople entering a private world of concentration just before competing. They are seemingly oblivious of everything and everybody around, focusing only on what they have to accomplish and the private thoughts that help them to do that. Sometimes little rituals help this concentration. But essentially they are consciously entering into a downtime state that will help their performance. Actors and other public performers may go through a similar process of withdrawal to get to their peak performance level, getting away from other people mentally if not physically.

To get into creative downtime:

➤ get away from the busy world of the here and now, and enter your private world of creativity;

➤ change your routines so that you have time to yourself every day, however briefly;

➤ cultivate your inner sensory world as you learn to recognise and trust the gentle, fleeting ideas it presents to you;

➤ use the techniques in Chapter 7.

WHEN TO TURN ON YOUR CREATIVE JUICES

In this second part of the chapter I will suggest some particular situations when you can apply these lessons and really benefit from a more creative, intuitive approach to what you are doing. How you react in these situations may mean the difference between mediocrity and peak performance.

When overloaded with information

Sometimes we are faced with so much information, whether so-called facts or opinions, that it is impossible to sort it out and come to a decision one way or the other. The left brain perpetuates this problem as it constantly looks at parts of the problem, so that it can analyse it. The more it hankers over the detail, the less it can see the whole picture. The right brain, on the other hand, thinks holistically and sees the situation as a whole or tackles different problems in parallel. In this mode you step back from the immediate problem and see things in perspective, and this is usually what brings the breakthrough. In this situation you need to:

➤ walk away;

➤ close the files up;

➤ tackle another task with a fresh mind;

➤ put the present task out of your mind until tomorrow, then see things in a fresh light;

➤ ask what are three top facts concerning the problem or situation.

When you don't have enough information

The other extreme is when you don't have all the information you need in order to make a sound decision. Obviously in such a situation you do what you reasonably can to obtain more relevant data. But at best this process is one of diminishing returns — you will never have all the information and, if you could get it, the extra effort would probably not be worth it. Moreover, in many cases you don't know how to get the information or even the sort you need. This is where the right brain does wonders and can make sensible deductions from the flimsiest of inputs. You may think of a person with just the knowledge you need. The right brain is the source of so-called feminine intuition, first impressions and gut feelings.

In each of these cases the quality of insights is not based on the level of information, but on the way it is synthesised by the unconscious mind. This right brain processing is a mental skill which takes practice. Your logical left brain is the perfectionist in you; your right brain knows how to make the best of a bad job. This needs a lot of trust in your unconscious mind, especially if you are not sensitive to gut feelings or hunches. Even trusting can become a habit and, as with any habit, it gets easier and eventually you don't have to think about it.

Prejudice or wishful thinking?

There are risks of course and some people hate risks. But note that there is a difference between true intuition and wishful thinking or off-the-wall ideas, or even straight prejudice, and this distinction is only recognised by experience. A little reflection will usually determine whether your ideas are pure fantasy or based on prejudice. Or an honest friend or relative might help.

In the case of intuition, external sensory inputs — the facts of the situation, if you like — may be missing. So you have to resort to internal knowledge; your interpretations or perceptions of sensory recordings of millions of external experiences in the past. These are the 'facts' upon which intuition is based. And, as we have already seen, insight will be based on the quality and breadth of this 'recorded' experience. This is too sophisticated a job to be done in the step-by-step, sequential way that the left brain processes things. So in these situations of sparse information, whatever the risks, you need to resort to intuitive thinking. So when you don't have enough information:

➤ mentally go over everything you know about the situation, and what you don't know, then let the matter go from your mind;

➤ be sensitive to insights as to what extra information you may be able to get easily;

➤ think about who you may be able to get help from;

➤ ask yourself what information you would like to have if you could get it;

➤ then ask yourself how your point of view or decision would change and how you might view the situation differently.

When in a crisis

We saw earlier that ideas do not come in a vacuum, but that they happen in response to some need, problem or desire — there is a purpose. A crisis, of course, quickly 'registers' on the brain as an important problem and outcome (unexpressed outcome or goal: 'to get out of the mess'), so there is plenty for the unconscious brain to work on. Accordingly, your bright ideas will tend to relate to the crisis, or perceived need, and your right brain will 'decide' what is priority. Faced with a life and death situation, the human mind becomes extraordinarily creative.

Nearer home, perhaps, if your job hangs on the successful resolution of a crisis, you may be surprised at your ingenuity at dealing with it. On the domestic front, if the bailiffs are due to repossess your home in ten days' time you will soon think of creative ways of lessening the imminent pain, and protecting yourself and your family. Old mindsets are jettisoned and you start to think of anything that might help. But the same rules apply: if you get so wrapped up in the problem that it fills your mind constantly, you will tend to spin your wheels and probably mentally blank out. The crisis becomes a drama or a nightmare. Whereas by getting your mind away from the crisis for a while, or just doing something else, whatever it is, to occupy your left brain, ideas will soon come. Know when to back off and rethink your outcomes and priorities.

Usually the creative brain cuts in automatically in response to a crisis, just as emotions such as fear precede instinctive actions. But how we react to these creative ideas will determine how we act and perform — what we achieve. They can be logically discounted, suppressed as far-fetched or just written off to an over-fertile imagination. Only when we trust and act upon insights can they be transformed into actions that will resolve the crisis and, in right brain style, find a 'silver lining'.

So here's how to deal with a crisis:

➤ Depending on any actual deadlines, take a few minutes or hours away from the crisis.

➤ Preferably sleep on it, having gone over all the pros and cons, possibilities and the very worst that might happen.

➤ Think about anything good in your life so that the present situation is kept in context.

➤ When ideas do come, don't waste them. In the absence of any logical solution (which crises don't tend to have) they are the best your mind can produce, so will provide your best (peak) performance in the circumstances.

➤ Don't give up, but give *over to* the part of your mind that is best able to help you through.

When you are in two minds

In some cases you may have formed two or more sound alternatives but still there remains the problem of deciding which is best. This may be a decision between two courses of action based on logical thinking — perhaps using different assumptions or data, or just listing pros and cons. Or, more likely, it is a dilemma between heart and mind. In other words you cannot decide between what is the logical way and what you instinctively feel should be done. This is the classical right brain/ left brain dilemma resulting from two entirely different mental operating systems producing different 'solutions'.

In a contest the articulate left brain will usually win and will not be inclined to acknowledge the 'right brain perspective', let alone fight the corner of its mute partner. The right brain and mid brain, or limbic system, is stuck with feelings that cannot even be expressed, so they are unlikely to stack up when you have to justify your decision to other people or give chapter and verse for your decisions. Only experience will convince you of the value of these feelings (how many times have they let you down?) and understand the form they take. But once skilled in holistic or bicameral (two-sided) thinking you will learn to be sensitive to those feelings whenever you are 'in two minds'.

So, when 'in two minds':

➤ relax and let you mind freewheel;

➤ think about what feels right;

➤ toss a coin, agreeing which alternative action heads and tails will represent. If you feel like tossing it again your subconscious mind is probably saying 'no', so go the other way. If you are happy with how it falls, follow that course of action. If you suddenly change your mind, follow your feelings.

None of these lessons requires a high IQ or any formal training. Using your creative mind involves simple common sense. But that is not to say that it will always come easy, because change is involved. It may not seem natural to stop trying if you have been in the habit of trying all your life. And the same applies to relaxing if it is not in your nature to relax. The important thing is that you *can* relax, be goal-oriented, see things in a different light, and ask questions. You can start to trust your intuition, at first in little things and then in any crisis and for the most important decisions. Start applying these simple lessons, one at a time, and make a note of the outcomes, including how you feel. In the next chapter you will learn how to turn pressure to your advantage.

5
TURNING STRESS INTO SUCCESS

People seem to perform better when the pressure is on, at least up to a certain level. When the pressure gets too much, however — and we usually refer to this as stress — performance crashes. This happens at different levels for different people. Some thrive on constant pressure, while others succumb quickly to the slightest change or setback. Provided we stay within our personal threshold and to some extent manage pressure, creativity and performance can actually be enhanced. In some 'success stories' pressure actually turns out to be a big motivating factor. In any event pressure, surely, is a universal fact of modern life. If welcomed as a resource you can turn what might have resulted in damaging stress into a positive aid to performance. An Old Testament writer got it pretty close: 'Man is born to trouble as the sparks fly upward'. We are stuck with it anyway, so the smart policy must be to use it rather than let it use us or even destroy us.

TURNING PRESSURE INTO PEAK PERFORMANCE

Some people will hardly get out of bed in the morning unless there is a pressing, motivating reason, while others require the slightest stimulation to operate at their peak. Top business people often date some of their most creative achievements to times of great pressure in the company. Jerry Swan, UK managing director of Caterpillar, said he came up with his best ideas when the company was in 'survival mode'. Similarly Archie Norman, boss of the Asda retail food chain, says he does his best thinking in a crisis. Something similar occurs in sport. How many times has a soccer club produced the results when everything was against them?

And some people positively thrive on major problems which most of us would find stressful. The same applies in a family situation when a crisis occurs, whether due to a sudden illness, accident, bereavement or financial trouble. Somehow people produce remarkable achievements which they would not normally have been capable of. These times invariably have their share of both eurekas and flow.

But there are as many examples of damaging stressful experiences. The deciding penalty shots in the 1990 World Cup proved to be the downfall of the England football team. Psychologically, they were in uncharted territory and all the instinctive skills of an ordinary Saturday game departed them. The pressure was too much and they had not, it seems, been coached to cope mentally with such an eventuality — in particular the confident state of mind needed. By their very nature you do not get many chances to practise for such one-off situations, and this applies to important job interviews or speaking to a large audience just as it does in sport. In some cases this is to do with self-image, which I cover later in the chapter. But to achieve unconscious competence in anything, and especially in stressful situations, does require the sort of repetition — practice — that creates habits. So you have to resort to *mental* practice, which I also cover in this chapter, and which can often be as effective as real practice, even assuming you had the opportunity for it.

The telephone-number financial rewards in modern sports such as snooker, tennis, golf and soccer add further to the pressure, especially in the critical final scoring. World number 1 golfer Greg Norman gave away six vital shots in the closing holes of the 1996 US Masters as he succumbed to the intense pressure of the occasion, having given away similar leads on earlier occasions. His victorious opponent Nick Faldo, in the face of the same pressure, exploited the situation as he remained calm and 'in the zone'. From whichever way you looked at it, pressure was a major factor in performance, at this world class level. Technical skill, years of experience and conscientious practice hardly came into the picture. But we all know that this is not just the case at top class level. Most of us face pressure day in and day out, and how we respond to it affects everything we do and what we achieve. Decide to get the better of it. It is only a matter of know-how.

Pressure and stress

Pressure is both inevitable and desirable. It is what life is all about. But it is a neutral force. It can produce both good and bad outcomes, depending on your ability and skills for coping or on what you are stimulated to achieve in the face of it. Pressure is an ongoing phenomenon that has got to be managed rather than solved with a one shot solution. Whether you are a welfare worker, professional footballer, fireman or stage entertainer, pressure comes with the job. Whatever sort of a day you have the chances are there will be more of the same tomorrow, so you will have to learn to live with it.

In business pressure can come from competition and the rapid change brought about by technology. In service jobs the worst pressure usually comes from people, especially difficult ones. In the new business age of delayering and subcontracting, job insecurity or actual unemployment bring their own pressures, almost regardless of the industry and nature of the work you do. The pressure that wrecks performance and even health is unpredictable and often ephemeral, and comes in 1001 guises, so no standard problem-solving technique will be of any use. Rather, you have to know your own optimal level and then manage your lifestyle in a way that capitalises on this inevitable life fact we call pressure.

When we go beyond the right level of pressure we experience stress, although the term is often used to mean pressure, in which case we usually refer to a harmful level of stress or *distress*. Such stress reduces effectiveness and produces some nasty physical and mental side effects as well. Pressure is universal — and as a fact of life it is not negotiable, although as we shall see it can be managed. Stress is negotiable. It's a choice you can make. The choice is in how you react or adapt to pressure. If you adapt positively you learn, grow and perform better — ultimately to your peak performance. If you do not adapt to pressure you experience stress and embark on the all too familiar downward performance spiral.

The big mistake is to confuse pressure and stress, and try to get rid of all the pressures. For example, a busy executive might pack in his job and retire to his dream farm in the countryside to get off the business treadmill. But in due course new pressures will replace old ones with things like the weather, new skills to learn, new relationships to forge, uncertainty, newly discovered health problems, family changes, getting older and — if he succeeds in truly reducing pressure — the inevitable stress of boredom or even worthlessness and guilt. So the answer is not to remove pressure, but to manage it — to use it, just like your time, a talent or any other resource.

Another mistake is to assume that we all respond to pressure in the same way. In fact we differ dramatically. One person gets relaxation and pleasure from the very activity that would cause another person debilitating stress. Simple sports and pastimes, like jogging or fishing, as well as the more daring ones like paragliding or bungy jumping, are subject to these very different perceptions.

More than that, a person's stress threshold changes depending on the kind of task they are doing, problem they are facing, decision they are making, or what time of the day or day in the week it is, or according to just how they happen to feel at any moment, or — and this can be critical — what other pressures they are going through at the same time. Even the most resilient person will succumb to a series of traumatic life events, such as a bereavement, a divorce, a house move or a job change, when they all happen at the same time. These pressures have a compounding effect in producing stress.

No technique or three-point solution can cope with this unpredictable, ubiquitous life fact we call pressure. Just like managing your health or your time, pressure requires ongoing management. But the payoff is huge in terms of performance. Pressure is one of the variables that most people have not tapped, simply because of a lack of understanding about its neutral role and its positive potential in affecting performance, or because they confuse pressure (the many outside forces working universally in all our lives) with one result of pressure not managed — stress.

Harnessing and regulating pressure

This is the bottom line: pressure produces peak performance. We work best when stimulated and stretched, not when we are bored and unmotivated. You just have to manage the level of . pressure, and harness it for greater motivation and better performance. The human fight or flight response is well known, but we also know the harm that unwanted chemical changes can do if not channelled into the physical responses for which they were designed. They still play a big role, for instance in sport, when the adrenaline burst can make the difference between a medal and mediocrity. Or, in an emergency situation, when a person walks a mile with an injured leg to summon help for a friend injured more seriously or lifts a car to free a child trapped underneath. And it comes into play in a less physical way when you need stamina to keep going to complete a project at work. This primeval chemical assistance affects the times of flow we have already discussed, when even your aches and pains are forgotten, and everything seems to be subsumed into achieving your goal. Peak performance draws on these basic, mysterious powers, as well as the knowledge and technical skills that seem so sterile by comparison.

Top performance today seems to be more mental than

physical, even in so-called physical sports. So if we are not to suffer the health consequences of inappropriate and potentially lethal chemical bombardment we need to manage the process, and regulate pressure to optimise performance. At one level this may mean changing your lifestyle. External circumstances, at least as far as they affect us, can be changed. You do have choices. You don't always have to say yes and you don't have to keep up with the Jones's. This is life management.

But there is another level. Pressure, as we have seen, is a matter of perception — how you view, for instance, different external circumstances, react to people's opinions, or set your values and priorities. These perceptions determine your response — in behaviour, achievement and performance. But you can change your perceptions by reframing situations and the techniques I describe in Chapter 8 will help you to do that.

Understanding the role of pressure will set you up for improved performance; being able to manage it sets you up for peak performance and marks you out as a true achiever.

Living in the zone

To get the better of any pressure that you face you need to learn about yourself rather than the textbook characteristics of stress and how the average person is affected by it. This is not difficult and you just have to keep a few things in mind.

As we have seen, the relationship between pressure and stress varies from person to person, situation to situation and from time to time. It involves how difficult or easy we perceive the task or goal to be, and how we perceive our ability to achieve it. This is illustrated Figure 1.

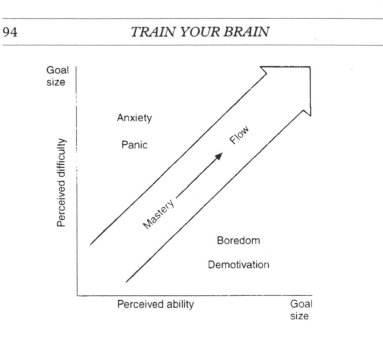

Fig 1. Level of pressure

This shows that there can be a problem at both ends of the graph. Too little pressure and you are bored and unmotivated, and are not inclined to do anything, let alone do it at your best. Too much pressure and you panic, 'freeze' in what you are doing and over a period suffer what is termed burnout, or a more serious mental or physical breakdown.

Paradoxically, at the first extreme, if there is not enough work to do or it is boring, undemanding and repetitive, stress can also result. The feeling of being wasted or under-utilised, or having 'missed out' in life, for most people, is especially stressful. So either extreme can cause stress. But, as we have seen, we are all different and one person can operate quite efficiently in the most mundane job that would drive someone else crazy.

The comfort zone

The comfort zone is just that — where you feel most comfortable. There is some challenge and stimulation, but you are not pushed. You obtain reasonable results and can maintain a balance with other parts of your life. Pressure may arise from time to time but on the whole you feel comfortable in what you are doing. With practice, even complex work becomes routine. From time to time you need some fresh challenge to keep you stimulated, but, to stay comfortable, you need it in small doses. You don't get ulcers or other stress-related illnesses in the comfort zone, but nor are you likely to set any performance records.

The stretch zone

The stretch zone takes you beyond this level. You start to feel the pressure and stimulation. You learn more, and grow more, in skills as well as confidence and self-esteem, so that you can face even bigger challenges. 'Experience' is speeded up. There are more mistakes but you learn a lot faster. Somehow you have the energy you need to stay in a resourceful, confident state. Experiences of flow, however enjoyable, are typically stretching experiences, such as a complex project or mastering a difficult skill.

The strain zone

Strain is when you are over-stretched and feel you are losing control. You do not get the same pleasure out of your work. Performance deteriorates and the upward cycle of growth turns into a downward spiral of stress. Fortunately there are usually warning signals and strain may result from a single, difficult task rather than the level of your main work. If you can just see 'light at the end of the tunnel' that may be enough to stay in control, provided you take time out to relax when the special job is put to bed.

The panic zone

This is when your world collapses and you just can't take any more. It can happen suddenly and by its nature there is no early warning. Something snaps and from that point everything you do is wrong or inadequate. Others notice and the organisation feels the effect as well as the individual. It's a dangerous state to be in and, although some executives seem to drive themselves on to such a state, it's the worst way to up your performance.

Your pressure-performance curve

Managing pressure for peak performance therefore means managing your own unique pressure-performance curve. We all have a different threshold. Even a pressure cooker has a limit over which it will overflow or explode. This means understanding how pressure affects you in different ways and at different times so that you can identify which zone you are in. Don't make the mistake, however, of thinking that you have to remove all pressure from your life. But, on the other hand, don't think that success depends on handling ever increasing amounts of pressure. It may seem tough and macho, but it is highly inefficient. Some say 'It is better to burn out than to rust', but the wiser adage is 'You need not succumb to either'.

As well as being different from other people, your personal pressure threshold will vary over a period, from time to time in the day or week and in different circumstances. For instance, there are things you take in your stride today that would have caused you a lot of stress a few years ago. These changes might come with a change of job, exposure to new places, people and experiences, as well as through stretching yourself in conscious, positive self-development. Any major achievement, or just getting through a crisis experience, can lift you a notch or two in your pressure performance curve.

In this light even negative circumstances outside your control can be treated as opportunities for personal development rather than an excuse for non-performance. You can positively and consciously increase your threshold, and cope comfortably with tasks that would previously have caused you stress. Alternatively, you will be healthily stretched in activities that would previously have caused you to panic. That is part of your pressure self-management.

The fact that you have changed in the past — whatever the circumstances — means that you do and can change in other areas of your life if you decide to do so. So over a period your threshold will get higher and higher as you get new confidence, and transfer this confidence in successes from one area to another. Because this happens incrementally — one little stretch at a time — you can rise to unimaginable heights of performance without suffering the downsides of harmful stress. Regardless of your individual achievements, the process of personal growth brings its own satisfaction. Just managing yourself in this way means success.

Constant pressure has a negative, cumulative effect, as we have seen. Your mind has to take time off. But, conversely, continual achievements, however small, have a positive, cumulative effect in taking you towards peak performance. And just as different kinds of pressure (like moving house, changing job and suffering ill health) can bring about overload, so a variety of individual achievements, in every part of your life, is equally beneficial to your success as a top performer. So there is no excuse for executive burnout, any more than there is for neglecting or misusing your physical body. It is just a matter of understanding and managing your personal pressure curve. Several of the techniques in Chapters 7 and 8 will help to get otherwise impossible tasks or problems into a manageable perspective, and even turn them round to your advantage.

Manage your personal pressure curve by:

➤ setting goals and objectives at a level that stretches you, and enjoying each success;

➤ lifting your sights after each achievement so that you maintain your motivation;

➤ trusting your intuition to come up with ideas and solutions.

Pressure and creativity

We have already seen cases in which creativity seemed to be increased as pressure mounted. The instinct to survive brings with it remarkable creativity. Some of the best entrepreneurial stories are those based on the demands of survival, perhaps in a different country, and in the absence of money, education and any omens of success. If your job or department is to be axed you start to think of all sorts of ingenious ways to prevent the downfall of the company, the parent group and modern society. Best-selling author Jeffrey Archer wrote his first novel to get out of financial ruin, so it had to succeed. I'm not suggesting that financial pressure will produce a best-selling novel for you, but it was a major factor in one person's success. The key is our attitude to the pressures that confront us, and how we respond to them and thus control their effect.

If we succumb to harmful stress the creative juices soon dry up. The panic zone doesn't produce great works of art, novels, scientific breakthroughs or peak performance — just panic. But the principle remains that the right level of pressure does wonders for your performance. The secret is in knowing your own pressure threshold and positively managing it to bring about success.

Many people find themselves creating pressure — perhaps by cutting it fine on deadlines or taking up challenging new interests with demands on their time — in order to get motivated and operate at their peak. For some people, on the other hand, tasks have to be broken down into smaller, manageable chunks, before they can be faced with confidence. Or in other cases skill training is undertaken before embarking on anything very demanding. In each case the 'pressure feeling' can be a helpful signal and in the end it can be an ally in achieving optimal performance.

YOUR PERSONAL PRESSURE TRAINING PLAN

Here is how you can turn any pressure round to help you perform to your best. Make it your plan and commit yourself.

Get pressure on the record

➤ Make a note of the kind of jobs and situations that caused you stress or panic in the past.

➤ Break down similar current tasks into manageable chunks you believe you can cope with.

➤ Make a note of tasks you know have to be done but you find boring and demotivating. Add some challenge — give yourself tighter personal deadlines, break your own record, think of better ways to do it or even eliminate the task, add some extra value so that you are stimulated with healthy pressure.

➤ Make a note of your pressure coping achievements, and congratulate and reward yourself.

Change your point of view

How you perceive any situation will determine how stressful it will be. By changing the meaning of something you will change its effect on you. You can start having some control simply by introducing more than one possibility or interpretation — 'Could this mean something else?' Mentally this gives you choices. The more creative you are the better you will be able to reframe a situation, the more choices you will give yourself and the more control you will achieve — at the very least over how you react and feel. Here are some more specific tips for changing your point of view.

➤ View stressful behaviour as the other person's problem and don't let it affect you.

➤ Don't bear grudges. You know who will be the loser.

➤ Mentally change the timescale. Imagine how you will feel about a stressful situation in, say, one year's time.

➤ Reframe the situation by changing its meaning or putting it into another context. In what context would this be acceptable or even enjoyable? Do you react to stress differently at work, at home and in certain social situations?

➤ Use the reframing techniques in Chapter 8 to tackle specific stressful problem situations.

➤ Imagine the worst scenario and think about the probability of that actually happening. Decide what you can do about it.

➤ Accept the worst mentally so it holds no further fears for you.

➤ Think of an optimistic outcome — a silver lining in the cloud.

Put things into perspective

➤ Write down the things that really matter to you and get the present situation into perspective. Don't things change when you are faced with a family crisis, such as when a child has an accident or a friend learns of a terminal illness?

➤ Decide on what you will allow to affect you and what is not worth the trouble. What would have to happen to make you start to assert your rights and pursue your own important interests?

➤ Prepare yourself positively for peak performance following the suggestions in Chapter 7.

See the funny side

➤ Start seeing the humour in stressful situations. This is a powerful form of reframe and a right brain skill you can cultivate.

➤ Have fun, as you did as a child. Studies show that nursery-age children laugh an average of 450 times each day; adults only 15. We learn better and achieve more when we enjoy what we are doing. Enjoyment is a state of mind you can induce if you really want to — whatever the outward circumstances.

Overcome worry with action

Use this four-part success cycle:

➤ *Decide what you want.* Make your goal positive: not just to get out of your stressful situation, but to achieve what you would prefer instead. Visualise clearly what you want rather than what you don't want — that's the right brain language of peak performance.

➤ *Do something.* Carry out the suggested actions given in this book. Make some of the changes suggested in Chapter 7. Make a commitment to what you have to accomplish by a letter, telephone call or by incurring a financial cost.

➤ *Notice what happens.* Develop 'sensory acuity'.

➤ *Be flexible* to change what you do.

This model applies to achieving any goal you like — it is a model for personal success — so don't just wait for pressures and problems.

Don't underrate yourself

Your self-image is the biggest single factor in your behaviour and achievements. Chapter 7 gives specific help here, but there are some simple things you can do straight away to improve your self-image:

➤ Watch your self-talk. We often run ourselves down and this can be a self-fulfilling prophecy that the subconscious brain takes as reality.

➤ Say positive, confidence-boosting things to yourself.

➤ Congratulate yourself and give yourself rewards.

➤ Look for the good points when you blow things.

➤ Check back (Chapter 3) on what your brain is capable of and decide not to waste it.

➤ Interpret what you do positively. If you do a good job, don't put it down to a fluke. If you fail, be more inclined to view it as a fluke or one off.

Slow down, relax

The rules for coping with pressure are much the same as the positive peak performance lessons based on the examples in Chapter 2. You recall that the imaginative right brain thrives on a relaxed state of mind and will not be rushed. Learn to relax:

➤ Give your right brain time to do its thing.

➤ Concentrate on achievement rather than activity.

➤ Be in a sufficiently relaxed state of mind to receive even the most subtle insights. Listen to your inner voice.

➤ Take up interests and hobbies that foster a slower pace of life, thinking and dreaming time, and creativity.

➤ Learn about breathing, posture and relaxation techniques (Chapter 7).

➤ Every day make at least one conscious effort to slow down all bodily movements — not just limbs but head and trunk as well. Make your movements deliberate and slow.

➤ If your job is rushed and stressful choose a holiday where you have to slow down. River or canal cruising with a speed limit of 5 miles an hour can be a great stress therapy and provide ample thinking time.

➤ Now and again arrange to get away from everyone and just stop what you are doing. You might fill the vacuum with reading a novel or doing something that you enjoy but never seem to get round to. Don't feel guilty about it. It's your life and this is an effective way to improve your all-round performance, not to mention the bonus of health and well-being.

Be yourself

A lot of stress comes from being unable to say what is on your mind when dealing with work colleagues or friends. The pent-up energy blocks creativity and performance, and will probably build up to bigger stressful situations. Although on the surface it appears that friendships are made by being cooperative and in agreement, in fact respect and long-term relationships are built on mutual honesty and assertiveness. Look at the section on self-esteem in Chapter 7. You are your unique self and you will always perform better in that role rather than play acting another character you aspire to be.

Be aware

This is half the solution, especially if you can anticipate future pressures before they have taken you by surprise. In other cases the pressure may be ongoing, its effect being more in the compounding effect it has rather than in individual events. This is the case when a certain individual always makes you feel angry, insecure or incompetent. In such cases it may help to keep a diary and record how you feel. Record any stressful event or circumstance over a period of days, including:

➤ *the date and time* — we may be more vulnerable to stress at different times of the day;

➤ *the situation* — sometimes a place has its effect on you, such as a conference room or noisy office;

➤ *your feelings*, including the physical symptoms such as dry mouth or churning stomach. It may help to rate the intensity of your feelings on a scale of 1 to 10.

This self-knowledge will turn out to be useful as you start to control the effect of pressure and reframe situations. Your perception will change. Your awareness and self-control is another measure of your personal performance on the way to excellence.

Know when to avoid

You always have certain choices when faced with outside pressures which cause you stress. Here are four alternatives:

1. Face up to it — stand and fight, if you like.

2. Run away or give in to pressure. Saying 'yes' when you mean 'no' is a popular form of this choice. In practice this means that you achieve precious little, as pressure comes with territory, and sooner or later you will have to deal with it.

3. Do your best to change the situation — starting with yourself and how you perceive it. This may also mean saying 'no'.

4. You can avoid pressure. This does not mean fleeing but rather seeing a conflict situation ahead and making sure you are not in the middle of it when it comes. Peak performance

is about being smart, not proving that you can handle any degree of stress or overcome any personal barrier. So think ahead. Give yourself enough downtime to think at all. Learn from past experience, especially where individual people are concerned. Never take a hiding for nothing.

Be assertive

This is the number 3 choice listed above. As you build up experience and confidence you will choose this option more and more. Here are some tips on being assertive:

➤ Don't take on other peoples' responsibilities (a stress recipe) unless it fits your own longer term aims.

➤ Don't say 'yes' when you mean to say 'no'. We often get lumbered with stressful situations because we are not prepared to say no or get control of circumstances before they have got control of us.

➤ Don't try too hard to please.

➤ Be confident in your own self-esteem, know your rights and start to say what you want.

Model on your best

Think back with pleasure to a time when you performed at your peak. Remember all the sights, sounds and feelings associated with your success. Vivid mental rehearsal will recall the confident state, which you can use as a resource any time. Chapter 7 covers this in more detail. As a habitual peak performer you will experience a lot more such times. Your aim should be to live in that state.

Practise mentally

Often the pressure comes because a situation is new or unfamiliar. Unless you do something regularly it is unlikely to happen naturally — that is, you will not perform with unconscious competence, which is what peak performance is about. Even professional footballers don't play in world cups many times — let alone get chosen to take a deciding penalty kick.

Fortunately, because of the way the brain works, you can practise mentally and train your brain. Under the right conditions, your brain does not know the difference between a real and an imagined event. So it treats vivid, repeated visualisation as the real thing, thus overcoming the unfamiliarity that is usually the cause of nervousness on the big day. For most of us, unfamiliarity accounts for a lot of the pressure we face and for the poor performance that comes from being too conscious or trying too hard. You are unlikely to freeze up when making a speech if you do this for a living or on a regular basis and the adrenaline rush that most public performers speak of usually helps rather than hinders their performance. Similarly if you are familiar with a particular competitive sport you will probably take a certain level of pressure in your stride that would badly affect a novice. But for all of us there are some occasions that we have not become familiar with, whether standing up to give a speech at a wedding or lining up for an Olympic sprint. And this is where mental practise is invaluable and is indeed one of the key mental tools of top performers.

Mental rehearsal is extraordinarily powerful in all sorts of situations yet it is easy and enjoyable. Simply run through the whole event or situation in your imagination, as vividly as possible, always achieving the outcome you want, of course, so that you are not 'practising' failure - which we do all too often in real life. You will find more help on visualisation and what is termed 'future pacing' in Chapter 7.

Training your brain to achieve peak performance is relative. It doesn't mean that you are the best in the world. You never arrive. Nor does it mean that you act like an automaton and are never affected by how you feel, with good and bad days. But it does mean that you are constantly raising your own standards of personal excellence and achievement. It is about being better today than you were yesterday and better tomorrow than you are today. It is in continually improving your performance against your standards. Don't go for a few memorable super performances, but aspire to becoming a peak performer. Think about being, not just doing. More than anything, it means being in control whatever the pressures.

There is nothing mystical or superhuman about peak performance, it just means you are responding to the world as a capable, resourceful and enthusiastic person who thrives on challenge and looks for opportunities. You make mistakes but you learn from them. You use your brain and innate talents. You accomplish what you know inside you can accomplish — no more, but certainly no less. You do not short-change yourself. Pressure? You will start to welcome it and take it in your stride.

6
MAKING YOUR OWN LUCK

There is another feature of creativity that keeps cropping up which does not have the negative connotation of stress, yet nevertheless is rarely treated as a resource. Often ideas and the special performance that flows from them follow some happy coincidence or positive set of circumstances — serendipity. But happy serendipity is too valuable a feature to write off as luck. It is an important feature of personal achievement that you can capitalise on. Of course we also get strings of what might be called bad luck, but these do not usually produce great insights and, understandably, we are more keen to forget them quickly than to use them for future creativity. It's those useful runs of fortune we want to capitalise on.

The most creative ideas, even those of historical importance, seem to come spontaneously and without effort. But ideas happen in the mind. Outside circumstances, on the other hand, we usually consider beyond our control. Yet they affect what we can achieve. But outside circumstances, or fate, can work for us as well as against us, and it is common for accidents of circumstance to produce remarkable insights that transform our performance. These are the sort of happy occurrences we usually put down to luck. But however these occurrences are explained or interpreted, they can contribute dramatically to achievement. They are part of peak performance. As you read the examples below you will probably think of 'happy accidents' or coincidences you have experienced yourself. Although some of the examples I quote seem inexplicable in any logical way, like the stories of eurekas we saw in Chapter 2, they none the less contain simple training plans that will help you to tap into this kind of serendipity as another route to peak performance.

SERENDIPITY

Starting a revolution

Galileo was resting on a wooden bench outside a lovely little Italian church near the leaning tower of Pisa. While he was sitting there enjoying the summer afternoon, he focused on something thousands of churchgoers had seen many times — a candle hanging on a chain, gently swaying in the breeze. Intuitively he worked out that the amount of time it took for the candle to swing back and forth was independent of the length of the arc. If it travelled along a short arc it moved slowly, if it travelled along a long arc it moved quickly to compensate. Although Galileo was not the one to build a pendulum clock, he suggested that others did so and soon timekeeping accuracy improved considerably. Other precision machines followed and soon improvements began to sweep across Europe in wave after wave. Some historians have credited Galileo's serendipitous observation with the spawning of the Industrial Revolution. Having made the observation, the intuition itself was remarkable enough. But just as interesting, and the question you and I need to address, is why one person notices such an innocuous thing when thousands of others would pass it by.

No one with a jot of intelligence would deny the element of chance in all our lives. But what deserves our attention is how we respond to what chance throws up. And, as we have already seen in Chapter 4 in the lessons in creative thinking, we can also do something about positioning ourselves in such a way that we are not so much at the mercy of outside events. To a large extent we can choose where we go, whom we associate with and so on. A post mortem on a major piece of bad luck usually reveals something we could have done to avoid or ameliorate the impact, or even to have turned it round to our benefit. Blind acceptance of fate means that we don't go to the bother of an honest self-appraisal, so our future positioning, timing and creative thinking never improves. It is easy to chalk up failures to fate and circumstance without stopping to think how we might have prompted them, let alone reacted to them. Top performers, more than anything else, take responsibility for their behaviour and achievements. By any measure, some of the greatest achievers have had more than their share of life's troubles, but their inner strength has been a match for any outward circumstances. We set needless limits on what we are able to achieve and miss countless opportunities to create our own luck. Heroditus said: 'All men's gains are the fruit of venturing.' Chance, including the genes you inherited, has its place. But it isn't a big enough place to stop a person achieving their best. That power lies entirely in yourself.

Think of three work colleagues or friends who specialise in hard-luck stories. Everyone knows people who think the world is against them, and how everything would be different if their luck changed. Then think of things these people could have done — behaviour in their own power — to have changed things for the better. Then do something more difficult and appraise your own attitude to fate and circumstance honestly, and decide what responsibility you have for hard luck outcomes.

Being 'lucky' is a self-fulfilling state of mind. It is all about expectancy, self-belief, sensory awareness, creativity and most of all having a sense of purpose. Washington Irving wrote: 'Great minds have purposes, others have wishes.'

Microwaves and sticking plasters

An engineer at Raytheon, assigned to work on a new piece of radar equipment, noticed that candy bars in his pockets melted when he was near active radar transmitters. Intrigued by this phenomenon, he went out and bought some popcorn, and found that radar beams could cook that too. Over the next few months he and his fellow engineers gradually figured out how to perfect the Radarange which is sold today in countless millions as the microwave oven.

In the early 1900s Earl Dickson worked for a company that produced most of the surgical tape being used by American doctors. Shortly before joining them he had married a woman who was just learning to cook on an old-fashioned wood-burning stove, so she got plenty of practice wrapping her hands with bandages when she got burnt. Worried about her whenever he was away from home, he began experimenting with ways for combining gauze pads and tape so that, when she was alone, she could bandage one hand with the other. Unfortunately, while his simple bandage kit sat around in the kitchen to await his wife's next accident, the tape dried out and the gauze became a bit dirty. After experimenting with various protective covers, Dickson found that ordinary crinoline did the job effectively. Soon his company, Johnson and Johnson, began to market a new product which they called Band-Aid. In this case marriage, burns and his work concerns came together in happy serendipity to produce a groundbreaking product that has affected all our lives.

However limited you feel your work or life is, there are always plenty of situations in which you can grow and achieve personal excellence. Opportunities are always there for the spotting. Conversely, once missed they may well be lost for ever.

Slime and sticktights

Alexander Fleming's story is much better known. He noticed that an old petri dish in his laboratory was contaminated with a foul, slime-green mould. Resisting the temptation to throw it away, he studied the mould's curious growth patterns to find an unusual ring-like structure surrounding the contamination at the centre of the dish. Something mysterious and quite unexpected was killing the microbes that were taking a nap on his petri dish. Later he discovered it was a powerful germ killer which might never have been discovered, had it not been for his observation, by the name of penicillin.

In 1948 Georges de Mestral was walking in the pleasant Swiss countryside. When he got home he noticed a clump of sticktights clinging tenaciously to his jacket. Wondering what made them stick so effectively, he pulled a few off and examined them under his microscope to discover that they were covered with tiny curved hooks that snared themselves in the loops of his winter jacket. His powerful curiosity, and a good dose of serendipity, led to the creation of what was to become a universal fastener with a myriad of applications — Velcro.

Everything around you can inspire. In a business context this can be restated to say that there are profits to be made everywhere you look if you are open to creative ideas — even in negative or annoying 'sticktight' circumstances.

Sneakers and silly rhymes

A young researcher accidentally dropped a beaker on the floor filled with a new industrial compound. Several days later she noticed clean spots on her sneakers where the fluid had splashed. Out of that accidental spill came a dirt repellent substance now marketed world-wide called Scotchguard fabric protector. Do your own post mortem on every 'accident' you have. Look for learning and meaning for you. If you really want to up your performance, do a post mortem on every failure.

Theodor Geisel listened mesmerically to the rhythmic sounds that came from the engine and propellers of the cruiser taking him from Europe to New York. Intrigued by the rhythms, he began writing silly rhymes to mimic the beats. More rhymes came to him and eventually he published a book featuring them, and built around the strange happenings a little boy imagines on the street where he lives. The book, entitled *And to Think I Saw it on Mulberry Street*, went on to sell 200 million copies. A generation of children would have been worse off had it not been for the serendipity of sea, sounds and silly rhymes. So listen while you watch. Use all your senses.

INCREASING YOUR OWN SERENDIPITY

Intuitive associations

The examples you have just read are not remarkable so much as lucky breaks, as in the way the people involved made intuitive associations between very different things or events, the kind of which any of us might witness. The fact that outside factors were involved, rather than dreams, daydreams or ideas that come from nowhere, just make them seem more fateful or lucky. In fact the luck was created by observant people who were also in tune with their intuitive mind. So if you fancy getting these kind of breaks the principles are the same as you learnt from the eureka and flow experiences I quoted in Chapter 2. Did you notice, for instance, that the people seemed to be in a happy, relaxed state, rather than pressured by work or matters of urgency? Earl Dickson did not get his idea in the Johnson and Johnson laboratories but in his own kitchen enjoying the company of his new wife. Fleming must not have been too tied up in his work for him to notice a petri dish that had been there for ages. Georges Mistral was basking in the pleasure of his country walk when the sticktights took on a special interest.

This is really a pleasant way to be at your best. Other eureka features, like the surprise element, applied also. Although seemingly dependent on circumstances and timing, serendipity is just another example of the creative imagination at work in whatever situation you find yourself, however adverse, unexpected or unfair.

Capture the unusual

If you want to start producing a bit of serendipity, another important lesson is to expose yourself to a variety of unusual experiences. You don't often get special insights from the familiar, as your brain is programmed to accept recognised patterns and has long since stopped wondering about them, or even noticing them. You can choose to adopt a lifestyle that courts rich and varied experiences, and be open to reading new things, going to new places and meeting new people. Just like a child with a new toy, for a while we can all be so much more curious, observant and enthusiastic. Out of this variety of experience will come prolific insights that otherwise would have been missed for ever — peak performance on a plate.

A book by Michael H. Hart, called *The 100: A ranking of the most influential people in history*, makes a provocative observation which supports the need for varied sensory exposure, a theme that keeps cropping up in the examples. He noted that almost every important discovery in history was masterminded by people who lived in cities! Although this might be of little significance today when so many of the population in the West live in urban areas, early in the eighteenth century only about 6 per cent of the population lived in urban areas. It transpires that many of history's most influential power brokers travelled from city to city during the formative years of their chosen professions, and at each new venue they were exposed to new and unusual ideas. Eugene Linden of *Time* magazine echoed Hart when he wrote 'Cities remain the cradle of civilisation's creativity and ambition ... the catalytic mixing of people that fuels urban conflict also spurs the initiative, innovation and collaboration that moves civilisation forward'. The city analogy, although fascinating, is not as fundamental as the exposure to new ideas and experiences, of which city life and travel were the vehicles. Other people fulfil the same requirement by wide reading, for instance.

What to do

Contrary to the stereotype, lucky people do things. And we can do a lot to harvest the unlimited supply of happy circumstances and 'outside' factors that can improve our own performance. After all, coincidences and serendipity will always be with us, so somebody is going to come out smiling. You can literally use your senses to tune into whatever is on offer. Think about the following:

➤ Expect happy circumstances and coincidences. They happen all the time, so you may as well enjoy your share.

➤ Don't expect 'bad luck'. You get what you think about a lot and can always prove yourself to be right. 'I told you so' might seem clever, but it is not the recipe for peak performance.

➤ Start looking and listening. Notice things and think about them.

➤ Watch out for creative opportunities all around you waiting to be identified and exploited. The more rich and varied your experience the more opportunities will arise.

➤ Question anything unusual and check it out.

➤ Reframe actions, events and circumstances, especially negative ones. Look for different meaning. Get another or several different perspectives. You can use some of the techniques in Chapter 8 to help you.

Long before I researched this book my earlier research for the book *Think Like a Leader* produced remarkably similar conclusions about the intuitive and creative skills in top business leaders. People don't change, and there is plenty of serendipity still around. A wise and varied life outside the business, and outside their own industry, as well as in special interests and hobbies seemed to provide the richness on which business leaders' prolific imaginations could work and translate into business success. Frequent travel was another factor that seems to reflect the city-to-city travels of their creative forebears.

Pressure has strong negative connotations because of its main symptom — harmful stress. Because of this we can easily miss out on one of the most powerful resources for creative thinking and peak performance. Serendipity, on the other hand, is invariably enjoyed and appreciated for the immediate benefits it provides. Yet it is rarely valued as a resource that can be created and used for positive outcomes. As well as being able to stimulate creative insights and flow as we saw in Chapter 3 (and you will find some techniques in the following chapters to do this), you can start to create a lot more happy accidents by enlarging your world and developing your sensory awareness. You can practise being observant, watching, listening, feeling and taking interest. In this way seemingly random, innocuous things will take on a special meaning for you, your goals and purposes. Having learnt how to turn pressure to your advantage, you can now start to make your own serendipity. We create our own serendipity by practising sensory awareness — watching, listening, feeling. With practice, even being lucky gets to be a habit.

The golfer Gary Player used to say 'The more I practise the luckier I get'. And generations of successful entrepreneurs insist that you make your own luck. Like the eurekas we saw in Chapter 2 serendipity has accounted for countless human achievements and altered the course of history. Happy accidents need not be written off as fate, or an amusing or mystical fluke for fortune. This is something that can be harnessed. Using the tips and simple principles in this chapter you can start to create your own happy serendipity, and transform it into creative insights and achievement. So whether life metes out pressure or pleasure, stress or serendipity, with the right understanding, attitude and skills you can harness these for peak performance.

7

GETTING INTO A CREATIVE STATE OF MIND

P eak performance is affected by many things, but most people agree that you have to be in the right state of mind. You have to feel right about what you are doing. And lots of things affect how we feel. As we have seen, when it comes to winning ideas, most of us receive far more inspiration in a place we find relaxing and secure than in the bustle of a busy office, when interruptions are likely. Most important business ideas, for instance, occur outside the company offices, and often in the evenings, or over the weekend. Many breakthrough ideas occur in the middle of the night and early morning is also a prolific time.

We all have different ways to get into the right state of mind or psyched up. Some prefer to bounce ideas off other people and value the synergy of a group, while others are more productive on their own. Others become super creative when confronted with a major problem or crisis, as we saw in Chapter 5, and it seems their creative genius is held in reserve for such important occasions. Many confess they have to be in the mood, although they are not sure just how to create that mood. Some writers and artists, for instance, can be at the mercy of how they feel, while others have learnt what for them personally gets the creative juices flowing. For most people, creativity seems to happen by accident and is not affected by trying harder. It is hardly surprising that our unique brain reflects the uniqueness of each personality, his or her background, likes and dislikes.

Fortunately you can do something about your state of mind and for that matter what you believe. You can think what you want to think. You can believe what you want to believe about yourself, and interpret your actions, strengths and weaknesses, achievements, and even outside circumstances and events as you wish. Lifestyle and behavioural habits are also within your control. This means that, while you cannot produce insights or flow experiences on demand, you can create the correct conditions in which ideas and flow are stimulated, and can harness them for better performance.

PREPARING YOURSELF FOR SUPER CREATIVITY

In this chapter you will learn how to prepare yourself for super creativity and top performance, and get into the best state of mind. This starts with understanding and applying the lessons we have learnt so far, based on individual examples of excellence and how our minds work. Importantly, it then involves translating these lessons into lifestyle — doing things differently, spending your time differently, perhaps having a different outlook and attitudes. Then there are techniques you will meet to change self-beliefs and state of mind that may be new to you.

Here is how you can prepare yourself for greater creativity, more extended periods of flow and the peak performance that will inevitably result:

1. Understand the conditions under which creative insights and flow occur, and change your lifestyle to fit those conditions better.

2. Change your self-beliefs so that they are aligned to improving performance continuously.

3. Learn the skill of getting into an empowering state of mind for the job in hand.

4. Learn the skill of stimulating creativity in specific situations.

We saw in Chapter 4 the conditions in which creative insights and flow occur. Here I will summarise some of these and suggest how they can easily be translated into lifestyle changes. I then describe how you can change disempowering self-beliefs into empowering ones that will support high performance. Having got your underlying self-belief aligned for high achievement you will then learn how to change your state of mind in the shorter term so that it matches whatever you have to accomplish. Chapter 8 then describes some techniques that reframe problems and stimulate your creativity in specific situations.

Creative thinking characteristics

In Chapter 2 we saw something of the circumstances that typically surround inspiration. Research into top performers, past and present, and in many different fields of activity, reveals some characteristics of creative thinking that are universal. Apply them to your own situation:

➤ We usually come up with more ideas when we are relaxed than when we are tense and worried.

➤ Creative insights and flow are more associated with pleasure than pain. That is, unlike conscious thinking that seems like very hard work ('I just can't think any more', 'My brain can't take it'), most people enjoy getting spontaneous brainwaves and find pleasure in periods of effortless high performance flow.

➤ In most cases of high creativity the person has come first to expect ideas, and trust their unconscious minds to produce them when needed. They believe in their own innate creativity and resourcefulness.

➤ Creative people have learnt to make room for this kind of thinking as far as lifestyle is concerned. For example, a person may have learnt that by relaxing more and getting away from things more often they actually become more productive.

➤ As well as trusting the 'system', they have also learnt to trust the insights and ideas they receive, and are inclined to act on them and translate them into peak performance. At worst they will consciously consider and evaluate them, rather than suppressing them or killing them at birth.

Performance self-appraisal

Think of situations in which these general conditions have applied to you. For example, when and where you do you get your best ideas? In what circumstances do you produce your best work? In which activities are you extra confident? Start to take notice of how and when insights happen, and when your performance reaches an effortless 'high'.

➤ What were the circumstances?

➤ What happened that morning?

➤ Whom did you talk to?

➤ What sort of words went through your mind?

➤ What mental pictures did you see?

➤ What triggered the 'high'?

➤ What had you been thinking about before going to sleep the previous night?

➤ Was there a problem you were 'sleeping on'?

From this exercise, and using the general conditions listed above, you can then re-create the conditions, if necessary changing your routine and lifestyle to capture more right brain experiences. You will thus change your state of mind, and be more expectant and sensitive to what your subconscious mind has to offer.

Lifestyle checklist

You can determine what changes have to be made by asking yourself simple questions, based on the lessons in Chapter 4 and the universal conditions described above. Here is a checklist:

➤ Do I have enough thinking time to myself? How can I make more?

➤ What interests and activities do I find relaxing, and how can I make more of these?

➤ What sort of things do I really enjoy doing and how can I do more?

➤ Do I see myself as creative? If not, is my negative belief justified, or just the result of my early conditioning and random experiences? How can I change a belief to something more useful and empowering?

➤ Do I trust the ideas I get, or criticise or suppress them?

➤ Do I act on hunches, gut feelings and out of the blue ideas?

➤ Do I find that people capitalise on ideas that I had already thought of?

➤ How can I have a richer, more varied 'experience base' from which creative insights are drawn?

You will think of more questions and opportunities for change from what you read in Chapter 4 and what you learnt about how the brain works in Chapter 3. It remains for you to decide what you are going to do and do it. Take one step at a time. Don't start acting on hunches that could jeopardise your career, company or important relationships. Start on low risk situations. But get practice at acting on instincts and insights, and start to evaluate their value over a period. Give each change a chance to become a habit. You will soon fall back into an old lifestyle if you do not repeat the new behaviour enough. On average, habits take about three weeks to change.

Be creative in being creative. Think imaginatively about time waiting, travelling or otherwise 'wasted', for instance, and see whether you can convert it into quality, freewheeling, downtime thinking. Work out ways during your regular day and week in which you can avoid interruptions. How might your journey to and from work be more creative? Could you create bigger, more motivating challenges that stretch you? Take on new interests. Acquire new skills. Practise doing a lot more in less time and use your own creativity to come up with ideas. Clearly visualise your goals — hearing and feeling as well as seeing — until they are as real as if they had already happened.

Become familiar with your thinking spectrum (Chapter 3). When in uptime, focus fully on what you are doing and do one thing at a time. But don't bang your head against walls; know when to drop an activity and let your mind incubate it. Never be ashamed mentally (and perhaps physically) to walk away. Rather than just tinker with things, be prepared to change your lifestyle fundamentally if you have been squeezing out important creative downtime.

Become familiar also with your personal threshold of pressure. Be ready to break tasks down into smaller, more manageable chunks or, conversely, to build in an added challenge. Look for opportunities that will stretch and motivate you.

Changing your routine

To be creative you will have to be ready to abandon entrenched mindsets and start to see things from different perspectives. You can change how you perceive things by doing things differently. Try the following:

➤ Change your route to work.

➤ Move some furniture around.

➤ Watch out for anything unusual.

➤ Act as if you were someone else — perhaps a respected mentor, company shareholder or an inquisitive seven-year-old child.

➤ Do things at a different time. Change regular appointments around.

➤ Do things in a different order. Do first the jobs you usually leave to the end.

➤ Eat something different.

➤ Look for new angles on things.

➤ Do things differently. Change your systems.

➤ Get up and go to bed at different times.

➤ Do something completely out of character. Notice how it changes how you feel and affects other people.

➤ Work to a different agenda — such as to make people happy, have fun, see the bright side of every situation or to write your autobiography.

Don't do all these things at once! Notice how each change affects your state of mind and behaviour. Expect to receive spontaneous ideas as you open up your whole brain.

CHANGING LIMITING SELF-BELIEFS

All these lifestyle changes affect our outward behaviour. We are very conscious about any change of routine and other people certainly notice the changes. But outward behaviour is just part of the story — the visible part of the iceberg, if you like. What really makes us tick, and affects our performance, happens below the surface in the form of how we feel, what we believe and the values we hold to. Although invisible, and often outside consciousness, these nevertheless have a massive effect on everything we do and achieve.

Identifying your self-beliefs

Deep down is what we believe about ourselves and this governs all our behaviour. There has got to be congruency. If you believe 'I'm no good at numbers', 'I am not good at ball games requiring coordination' or 'I'm hopeless expressing myself in writing', I can just about guarantee that in each of those areas you will fall a long way below your potential. These beliefs simply become reality. More all-embracing beliefs such as 'I'm basically unlucky', 'I'm not really a creative person' or, at the extreme, 'I'm a loser' guarantee failure in lots of areas. In each case an efficient, but severely disempowering downward spiral has been created — probably years ago and without any rational basis. Every interpretation of every behaviour ('That's just like me' or, if you happen to do well, 'That was a fluke') just confirms the belief and reinforces the self-fulfilling spiral. Conversely, a single positive belief such as 'I tend to achieve whatever I set my mind to' will do wonders in all parts of your life and will be similarly a self-fulfilling spiral. In this light nothing happens by accident. Every behaviour is based on belief systems and values, even though in most cases we never give these a thought from one year to the next. So when change is made at this neurological level, its effect is usually dramatic. Each empowering belief is worth a fortune. In terms of personal achievement it is the bottom line. Self-beliefs are the barometers of all personal achievement and belief change know-how is the key to peak performance.

The first job is to identify your self-beliefs, and close friends or relatives who will be frank with you might save you some time. We are not in the habit of thinking about these beliefs which usually operate at an unconscious level. But here is one way to identify negative self-beliefs. Think back to a few experiences of what you consider failure, or cases in which the memory gives you displeasure. For instance, you may have succumbed to nerves in an interview, lost a sale, had a mental block or performed well below what you know you are capable of. While thinking about each experience, write down the beliefs about yourself, other people, work, or life that could have had a bearing on your performance. In practice these will tend to be your interpretation of the event. Using the example of an interview that went badly, you might list:

➤ I always think of things I should have said afterwards — I'm no good at thinking on my feet.

➤ I get nervous in any formal situation.

➤ My accent lets me down.

➤ The job was a bit above me anyhow.

➤ I didn't want the job badly enough — I'm not sure what I do want.

➤ I could have prepared better (or I prepared too much).

➤ I don't like blowing my own trumpet.

Some of these, like 'I get nervous in formal situations' can go straight on to your list and others can easily be restated as negative self-beliefs, such as 'I tend to underrate myself'. By carrying out the procedure for different situations — not just work-based ones — you will probably find that the same beliefs crop up repeatedly. In other words, you have a standard set of interpretations or excuses for your behaviour and performance.

As well as memories, you can use future situations that you will or may face, such as a specific upcoming meeting at work or important social event, imagining what might go wrong. The process works the same and you will experience the same sort of negative emotions as you would when recalling a past event.

Initially make as long a list as you like — it's all useful self knowledge. You can choose those you think have the biggest negative effect on your achievement, are the most irrational (dating back, perhaps, to your childhood) or crop up most frequently. A final shortlist of maybe three or four can then be used for the belief change process I describe below.

In the previous examples I did not include positive beliefs. For example, you might have said 'I usually do well under pressure', 'I enjoy talking about myself', 'That particular interview was a fluke — it was not like me at all' or ' I learnt so much from the experience.' The rule for positive self-beliefs is simple — leave well alone. It's great for your self-esteem to identify them, but you don't have to change them. A positive belief is a self-perpetuating spiral and you feed on your successes. But negative self-beliefs have to be handled ruthlessly.

Choose a self-belief from your shortlist that you would like to change (make the changes one at a time, as a single change can have quite a fundamental effect on your behaviour) and decide what belief you would like to put in its place. This might be a simple reversal — so, for example, instead of believing you are not creative, you now believe you are. Or you can go further, making the new belief whatever you want it to be. For example, 'I am at ease with people at any level and can express myself assertively' or 'I can quickly learn any new skill and easily adapt to change'. Go for a belief that will support present goals. In each case you have to be convinced that the old belief has no rational foundation, but that is not usually difficult and you don't need to kid yourself.

For instance, it can easily be established that we are not born with genetic shortcomings that prevent us from drawing a straight line (negative belief: 'I can't draw a straight line'), speaking in public, expressing ourselves in writing, learning new skills and so on. Nurture rather than nature has played its ubiquitous part. Even a random comment from a parent or teacher ('You can't sing to save your life' or 'You are so natural when it comes to dealing with people') can start a lifetime spiral in one direction or the other. Most of our beliefs are generalisations about our past, based on interpretations of painful and pleasurable experiences. As we saw earlier their basis is on your interpretations rather than the reality of experience. And as rational adults we are free to interpret experience or give it a meaning in any way we want to. It is a good idea to make these new beliefs useful or empowering — in other words the sort of beliefs that will help rather than hinder you from achieving what you want to achieve. So start with your goals and choose beliefs that support them.

Exposing negative beliefs

Sometimes we are the last to recognise the beliefs that underlie our behaviour. But, more likely, having identified self-beliefs, we underestimate their effect on our behaviour. Start to see your negative beliefs for what they are, and the damage, pain and embarrassment they have caused you. Associate them with pain, because the mind always seeks to steer clear of it. In thinking of negative experiences as I have described above, identify each negative belief with the pain and hurt it has caused you on different occasions. This puts a new light on seemingly harmless self-beliefs and the negative self-talk they generate. Logically, you will be ready to dump some beliefs.

Then ponder a real success and identify the supporting positive self-beliefs. It may have been in an area where you are particularly confident or 'gifted', such as in a sport or hobby, selling, handling difficult people or whatever. Associate them with the pleasure and success they bring you, but otherwise leave well alone.

To strongly associate your negative beliefs with pain ask yourself the following questions for each negative self-belief you identify:

1. In what way is this belief irrational, ridiculous or absurd?

2. What might this belief ultimately cost me?

3. How might this belief affect my relationships, health, career and well-being?

4. What might be the financial cost of holding onto this belief?

5. Was the experience or person on which this belief was based worth investing so much of my life?

Changing a belief

Here is a technique to change a disempowering belief adapted from my book *Masterstroke* (Piatkus, 1996) about the mental side of golf. It can be applied to any performance, whether sport, work, or personal goal. It is based on two important facts:

1. There is a two-way relationship between our beliefs and our behaviour. Beliefs affect our behaviour, but our behaviour in turn affects our beliefs. Change either and the other will change.

2. What we imagine intensively has the same effect on our brain as if it had actually happened. With enough emotional intensity and repetition our nervous system actually experiences the inner sensing as real. So as far as your brain is concerned, you can create experience.

This technique uses behaviour rather than belief as the variable, but rather than tackling external behaviour — the visible part of the iceberg, if you like — it creates behaviour internally to support your desired belief. As well as effectively changing a long-standing belief, this will have a fundamental effect on your behaviour, attitude and feelings.

1. Identify the disempowering belief

First identify the negative self-belief you would like to change. Go for one that is not too general (like 'I am a loser' or 'I am usually unlucky') nor too specific (like 'I always go to pieces when John attends the quarterly budget meeting'). But a belief about a particular kind of work situation, group of people (like bosses or clients), a nuisance habit you have developed or how you react to criticism is fine for this purpose. Write your belief down so that it is quite clear to you.

2. Decide on an empowering replacement belief

You then need a replacement belief. All your beliefs have served you well in their own way, as sort of survival rules. Your mind does not like a vacuum, so state the belief you would like to replace the disempowering one, and again write it down. A fundamental belief change has more potential power than a new computer programme or technical skill.

3. Choose three supporting behaviours

Then think of three behaviours that illustrate your positive belief — that is, things you would actually do if you really believed what you want to believe. You might go for experiences such as receiving a trophy or other accolade of success, including visualising the hearty congratulations of friends, the completion of an important work project, closing a sale, attaining an academic qualification or repairing an important relationship. Choose behaviours that can be realistically imagined using all your inner senses — sights, sounds and feelings — which act as evidence of the truth of your belief.

4. Mentally rehearse your new behaviours

Using your three examples, mentally rehearse each one in vivid detail; see yourself in your mental picture excelling in whatever way you want to. Initially stay outside the action, so that you see yourself as if watching it from outside (this is termed 'dissociated'). If you are not completely happy with your new performance, run through it again and fine-tune it wherever you wish, until it perfectly confirms your positive belief. Then put yourself right inside and experience everything as you actually would, including the reactions of other people, this time seeing things through your own eyes (termed 'associated'). In particular enjoy all the surrounding feelings and emotions, including the reactions of friends and colleagues that accompany your success. By repeating the visualisation as a form of mental practice, you will create the necessary internal behaviour that will support your new belief.

Applying this technique to your shortlist of offending negative beliefs, you will remove long-standing barriers that will free you mentally to achieve your best. The above is just one example of a belief change technique. If you want to try a different method, a longer technique, described in my book *NLP for Managers* (Piatkus 1996), makes the change through several stages, and may be more effective in the case of particularly long-standing beliefs.

CHANGING YOUR STATE OF MIND

Having made common-sense changes to your lifestyle based on the general conditions that support high performance, and aligned your beliefs, it remains to be able to get into the right state of mind when you need to. Every outstanding writer or artist has bad days, or might even dry up for long periods. And similarly top sportspeople with mega confidence can strangely go to pieces in particular circumstances for no known reason.

Relaxation and alpha waves

I have already referred to relaxation as one of the universal conditions that help creativity. There are plenty of ways you can relax and fortunately this is a skill you can learn, then continuously improve upon. The more of your life that is given over to relaxation and the better you are able to control your state of mind the more you will be able to harness your creativity. The time just before going off to sleep when you are physically relaxed but mentally alert is a time of special creativity. This is when the brain is ticking over at slow alpha wave rhythms between around 8 and 14 cycles per second. This is an important brain state, and one worth cultivating. It is associated with relaxed awareness. The mind is tranquil yet receptive. This brain state is also associated with pleasurable activities, better learning, and mental and physical control. In simple experiments volunteers with no previous training were able to control their minds to the extent of entering and sustaining an alpha brain state. This is done using simple feedback, such as a bell ringing when the alpha wave state is reached. People who have learnt meditation, yoga or a similar mental discipline typically produce the most alpha and can usually do so with little difficulty. But in fact it is a natural talent we all have and can be developed with practice. Essentially, it is knowing how to relax.

Relaxation techniques, about which there are plenty of specialised books, tapes and courses, will help you to get into such a state whenever you want to, and so take more control over your thoughts and actions. In particular it is a state in which your visualised goals are 'registered' in the brain. Vividly sensed these become the targets to which your automatic cybernetic, or goal-seeking behaviour is continuously and unconsciously steered.

Relaxation exercise

You can easily train yourself to relax. Set aside twenty minutes or half an hour during which you will not be interrupted. Sit or lie down in a quiet room — it doesn't matter what position you adopt as long as you are comfortable and can maintain that position for the whole practice period. You may wish to turn the lights down. If you are sitting, uncross your legs and rest your arms by your side. If lying down, lie on your back, with your knees raised and a slim cushion (or a book) to rest your head on. Play some calming music if you find that helps.

Close your eyes lightly, and keep your breathing light and

steady. Each time you breathe out repeat the word calm or some other word that helps you to relax, and imagine all your worries and tensions flowing out of your body. Now concentrate on each group of muscles. First tense the muscles of your fingers, wrists and forearms — make clenched fists, as tight as possible, a few times before you relax them. Imagine all the stress flowing out of your arms through your fingers.

Focus on your breathing, repeating your calming word each time you exhale. Next press your head hard against the cushion or chair back to tense your neck muscles. Hold for a slow count of five then relax. Hunch your shoulders as hard as you can, lifting them upwards and away from the chair back, and again count slowly to five before completely relaxing. All the time keep your breathing light and regular, and repeat to yourself your calming word.

Next tense the muscles of your jaw and tongue by clenching your teeth, pressing your tongue against the roof of your mouth. Close your eyes tightly and screw up your forehead. Count five slowly for each tensing then completely relax, feeling the tension leave each part of your body. To relax your torso, inhale as hard as you can until your chest will not expand any further, and at the same time flatten your stomach as though anticipating a blow, and again hold your breath and stomach tension for a few moments. Do the same for your legs, ankles and buttocks. Point your toes, stretch your legs and squeeze your buttocks. Maintain this 'stretch, point and squeeze' for a slow count of five, then enjoy the relaxation as you continue light breathing and imagine all the tension flowing out of you.

Notice the freedom from tension throughout each part of your body and the calmness as you repeat the word each time you exhale. If tension comes back to any part of your body, repeat the exercise. Start to recognise and enjoy the specific feeling of relaxation you are creating. After a while you will be able to use shortcuts to relax quickly anywhere and at any time. Just tighten all your muscles for as long as you can, deliberately slow down your breathing, and recall the experience of total relaxation you feel in your longer exercise.

Getting rid of 'busy' thoughts

Even when you are physically relaxed your mind might stay busy with thoughts. You can remove unwanted thoughts and calm your mind by visualising a pleasant place where you feel happy and safe. This might be a real or imaginary place, outside in nature or a favourite room and chair. Change the circumstances however you like until the conditions are perfect. As well as seeing things inwardly, hear the sounds and capture all the feelings until the experience becomes very real. Hold that beautiful state for several minutes and savour the total calmness. If thoughts come into your mind, don't fight them. Just calmly refocus on all the pleasant sights, sounds and feelings in your 'special place'. Don't worry if you cannot capture these internal images. Some people have difficulty in seeing things inwardly. But the chances are you had plenty of imagination as a child and just need a bit of practice to regain what is a universal human skill. In extreme cases you may have to start with visualising something you have just seen externally — such as the layout of the room you are in. Or use familiar subjects such as the face of a person very close to you. Then extend to past holidays, memorable enjoyable events such as when you received a prize or some accolade of success. You will rediscover this mental skill just as you regain fitness after having an arm or leg in plaster for a long time. Before long you will be able to explore distant childhood memories. The bad ones can be manipulated as you wish (a memory is just an electro-chemical pattern or brain imprint which is likely to change in some way every time we recall it in the light of more recent experience and values). The good ones can be used as resources to empower you to achieve your present goals. You may, for instance, be able to recall a time when you were completely relaxed and uninhibited as a child, and use this as a pattern for your present needs.

You may have to practise the techniques a few times until you can easily get into a state of physical and mental relaxation. In a short time you will be able to physically relax quickly, using shortcut methods. Then, as you become familiar with your inner special place, you will be able to reach it quickly and get rid of busy thoughts. These are skills just like other skills that require practice and familiarity. Every time you use them you will change how you feel and be empowered to do what you would otherwise not have risen to.

Instant alpha

In many cases you will have to get into an empowering state of mind quickly, with little notice. If you are summoned to the boss's room, for instance, you won't have time for the extended relaxation exercise above. But it is possible to 'anchor' the alpha state you have learnt to experience and to enter it more or less instantly. An anchor is anything that brings about a behaviour or state of mind — such as an alarm clock ringing in the morning, a certain voice or any sort of ritual we go through in order to perform better. A kinaesthetic anchor involves touch, or a physical gesture like crossing your fingers. An auditory anchor is any sound, such as a tune or words you might say to yourself when psyching yourself up like 'Go for it' or 'You can do it'. A visual anchor is something you see which triggers a certain behaviour or feeling — such as a spider, the office door of a top client or boss or an internal image such as one of your late grandfather. By associating specific, unique anchors with your alpha state, you can recall that state just by 'firing' the anchors. For example, you might visualise the calm scene you used in your relaxation exercise, crunch up your left big toe and say to yourself 'Calm, calm'. If these are strongly associated with your alpha state — fire them at the moment in your exercise when you experience the deepest state of relaxation — you will recall that state instantly. You can fire all three anchors, or, with practice and trust, just one of them (the kinaesthetic one is usually the most powerful). It is important for you to choose anchors that have meaning to you.

Another effective approach is to associate the alpha state with numbers. As you go through an extended relaxation exercise count downwards, say from 100. Time it so that by the time you reach 3 you are completely relaxed physically, and always associate this number with physical relaxation, preferably visualising the number 3 in a memorable way — it could be in bright lights or in gold copperplate script on an ivory card, for instance. Or you might create a movie, seeing yourself writing the number. Having got rid of busy thoughts by visualising a pleasant restful scene, as I described above, you can associate this state of mental relaxation with the number 2 — again giving that number special unique qualities that are easy to recall. The deepest state you can achieve, which will inevitably be at alpha brain waves, can then be reserved for number 1.

With a little practice you will be able to achieve alpha using a shortened countdown — say from 10 to 1, or even 5 to 1. In this case the numbers act as anchors, just like the words or physical gestures in the first method. In due course the association will be completely habitual and you will automatically enter alpha state when you visualise (and preferably hear and feel in some way) the numbers in your special way. In this alpha state you can carry out all sorts of mental activities, such as recalling and manipulating memories and internalising goals.

Add your own ideas about relaxing. Some people like to listen to music or tapes of natural sounds, such as waves on the seashore or a rushing stream. Some imagine being very heavy, and others being very light and floating away.

Planning for a better state of mind

Having learnt a relaxation technique that works for you, you can then do a lot in terms of your lifestyle to build in as many relaxing activities as you can. We all relax in different circumstances and ideally you will create more downtime without encroaching on the important things in your life, for instance by using travelling or other 'wasted' time for productive creativity. Some car drivers find a long journey on their own very relaxing, even in difficult traffic conditions. The pleasure they get and the level of unconscious competence they have achieved means that there is no stress and they can safely let their minds 'freewheel'.

Others find little pleasure or relaxation in driving and are non-creative at such times. Similarly, if cooking is a chore, you are unlikely to come up with right brain insights as might someone who gets pleasure and relaxation out of preparing a meal. On the other hand you might get the same sort of pleasure and mental calmness fishing, walking, embroidering or making models. So it's horses for courses, but somehow you have got to create the conditions for better quality thinking.

So, without any special training in relaxation techniques you can condition yourself to more creativity simply by ordering your lifestyle to include pleasurable interests and hobbies. The extra time you spend doing things you enjoy should be more than repaid by the time you might have spent stuck on frustrating problems. For the busy executive this is sound advice on health grounds as well as in terms of the greater creativity and productivity that naturally follows. If such times are crowded out by a workaholic lifestyle, don't expect to receive 'whole brain' ideas that set you apart from the crowd and give you the competitive edge in business. Quantum improvements, whether in your personal or business life, are rarely achieved through an intensive, uptime, usually blinkered lifestyle. The left brain is fine for reactive operational work, firefighting or work of a routine nature without too many variables including people factors. Proactive thinking that can cope with any degree of change and can spot opportunities rather than just react to known problems requires whole brain thinking of a higher calibre. The examples of scientific and entrepreneurial breakthroughs given in Chapter 2 illustrate just how extraordinary such thinking can be and its impact.

Note which of your activities help you to relax, and when and in what circumstances you tend to be creative. Keep a journal if you find this helpful, in which you can also make a note of any ideas you get. Then adjust your lifestyle to make room for more of such activities or new ones you equally enjoy. If such activities and interests do not exist, start making space for them, perhaps embarking on a hobby or interest you once resolved you would take up 'some time'. If this creates a genuine time problem, you may have to reassess your priorities, which is what the best time managers are doing all the time. Remember, however, that a few good ideas during a relaxed, creative spell can be applied to the most intractable time problems.

Creating creativity by mental rehearsal

Visualisation techniques can also be used to induce a creative state of mind. Think of a time when you were very creative, then spend time dwelling on the sights, then sounds, then feelings associated with the activity or event. Do this in a relaxed way using, if necessary, the 'alpha' relaxation technique described earlier to prepare yourself.

Then take it one stage further. Notice the characteristics of the sights, sounds and feelings you recall. For instance, a visual image might be clear or unfocused, black and white or colour, framed in a screen or panoramic. Or, in your mind, you might see yourself in the picture or alternatively be looking as if through your own eyes. These thought characteristics are termed submodalities, the modalities of thought (or representation systems) being your three main senses — seeing, hearing and feeling. Do the same for the sounds you recall — loud or soft, for example, or in the case of human voices, high or low pitched, fast or slow. Then do the same for feelings — note whether they are soft or hard, rough or smooth, and also any physical sensations associated with your super creative state of mind, like the tingling sensation sometimes attributed to music.

If you think back over different times when you were creative, the circumstances may well have been very different. For instance you might have a mixture of work and personal examples. But as you carry out the visualisation exercise you may well find that the submodalities are common. That is, there is a particular combination of thinking characteristics which, for you, means a creative state of mind. This combination or state can be called up whenever you need it, but you need to plan ahead for such an occasion.

Here's how to do it:

➤ Think of a time in the future when you would like to be creative. Choose a real opportunity, say a forthcoming work project, meeting or presentation.

➤ Imagine or mentally rehearse the situation or event using each of the three main modalities, and note the submodalities as you have just done with the creative memory.

➤ One by one, replace the submodalities with those you identified in your creative memory. In particular, if in your creative memory you saw things as if through your own eyes, whereas in the future visualisation you could see yourself in the picture, switch to the associated mode as in the empowering memory.

➤ Retune your future experience just as you would tune the picture and sound on your television for perfect reception.

Using this technique from NLP you can recall any state of mind you have known in the past and use it for positive purposes. It can also be applied to the state of flow we have already discussed or a time of special peak performance that was not necessarily associated with creativity, but perhaps with physical skill or dexterity, high focus and concentration, or a very strong desire or dream you were striving towards. You are simply modelling excellence, in this case your own. So isolated occasions of super performance can become more frequent and your overall level of competence more consistent.

The Disney strategy

Many people get good ideas but they seem to be quashed before they are given proper consideration. It seems that the logical left brain does its criticism and judgement before right brain ideas have had a chance to surface. The problem then is not that we are not creative, but that we need to learn to isolate each type of thinking. Neurologically, we need to let each side of our brain do what it does best. Sometimes, for example, we need to be practical and well organised, sometimes constructively critical and at other times simply generate ideas. This technique helps to separate three aspects of our thinking personality: the dreamer, the pragmatist or practical organiser, and the critic or judge. By separating the contribution each makes, each is maximised. The following description is adapted from my book *NLP for Managers*. The technique is based on work involving Walt Disney carried out by Robert Dilts, author of *Strategies of Genius* Volume I (Meta Publications).

1. Think of a situation or issue you would like to handle effectively. Make sure it is a real one — perhaps a personnel matter at work, a task which is complex and risky, or even intractable, or an opportunity you want to exploit — so that you give the technique a real test. Then allot three imaginary places in front of you which you can step into to represent your dreamer, your realist and your critic.

2. First, think of a time when you were really creative, and you came up with plenty of new ideas and choices. You can think back to earlier jobs or to non-work situations. Step into the dreamer position and relive the experience. Go through each modality, then bring the sights, sounds and feelings together so that you become in effect what you then were. The place you step into simply anchors that experience. If you cannot think of a time when you were creative, put yourself in the shoes of someone you know who is and imagine what they would feel like. Then step back from the creative position.

3. Next, think back to a time when you were realistic, careful and well organised. This may have been when you put a plan into action, handling the many practical aspects effectively. You can similarly draw in your imagination on others who display this strength. When the state 'peaks' in your mind step into the realist position, anchoring your state to that physical spot, then step back out.

4. Then become your critic, thinking back to a time when you

made constructive criticism, spotting the weakness in the arguments or solution. If you find this difficult, there is probably no shortage of critical people you could imagine thinking like. Step into the critic place, fully relive and anchor the experience, and step out again.

5. Now you have anchored these three states in the different locations, you can start to consider the actual situation in which you want to perform well. Step into your dreamer position and come up with all the creative ways you can imagine to solve the problem. Don't be side-tracked by what is feasible or sensible — just let the ideas flow unheeded, in brainstorming style, calling on the empowering creative state you have just experienced. In this state there is no criticism or even evaluation, so no idea will be put down. You can use language patterns such as 'What if ...', 'I wonder if ...', imagining what you might come up with if you were guaranteed success. This can be a pleasant experience, so enjoy your daydreaming and get to know your creative location just like a favourite chair or room. When you have exhausted your creative ideas, step out of the position and 'shake off' that state.

6. Then step into the realist position and put your ideas into action. Think of all the practical considerations, such as timing, resources, things you will have to organise and initiate, until the ideas make sense. Ask yourself 'How can I do this?' and answer your own question in a pragmatic, realistic way. Say it all out loud. If you have a partner, he or she can take notes and remind you of what you have to address later in the technique. Then step back out of the position.

7. Next, step again into the critic position and this time use your critical skills to come up with all the snags. What have you forgotten? What might go wrong? What is the payback? Don't pull any punches, be as critical as you like, while staying constructive and always bearing in mind your out-

come — the problem you are solving. Then step back into a neutral position.

8. Now return to your dreamer place, to think of more good ideas, this time addressing the practical problems and criticisms that have been made by your other 'parts'. Be just as creative in responding to barriers and shortcomings as you were when thinking of the initial ideas.

9. Continue to go through the cycle until your problem has been solved. You will probably find that one by one important weaknesses are solved — in effect becoming new problems — and that there is no limit to what your dreamer can think up when left to do the job without premature criticism. The critic will have fewer and fewer genuine criticisms but they will become more specific and can be addressed creatively. The realistic organiser will help to make each amended solution a practical reality. These three roles, while displaying strong identities of their own when anchored to their respective physical position, will begin to work more and more in harmony.

You now have the knowledge and skills to get into the right state of mind for creativity and peak performance. The following chapter describes a range of techniques you can use in different circumstances, but for specific goals or problems, to stimulate creativity and flow. Try them out. Train your brain. Use them in real-life situations to solve problems or create opportunities in your life. Peak performance is now within your reach.

8
TECHNIQUES TO TRAIN YOUR BRAIN

INTRODUCTION

You cannot produce human creativity to order by using techniques, any more than you can program a computer with imagination or humour. But some methods have been developed that help to foster or stimulate your innate creativity. There are dozens of such techniques, many of which have been used successfully in large companies around the world. Here I have selected a few you can use in different situations, and which I have used personally and in seminars and workshops internationally.

Decide on the areas in which you want to improve your performance. Think of three things that are stopping you from achieving what you want and treat these as problems, applying one or more of the techniques in this chapter to them. Start with blockages in your self, which are more controllable than outside factors and more likely to be the root cause in any event. For instance a person might have a negative effect on you, and you know quite well that they are not affected in the same way, or are even aware of how you feel. In the first instance, at least, the problem is yours and, as you learnt in the previous chapter, there are things you can do about it.

You can use the same techniques, however, to excel at something you are already good at. The process applies at any level. You can also address your performance in terms of goals remaining unfulfilled. You will see how you can easily relate 'problems' and 'goals' below.

It is always tempting to go for a mechanical process or technique rather than think for yourself. None of these techniques can be used without thinking and creative thinking at that. Having said that, nor can they replace the important principles about lifestyle and self-belief you read about in the last chapter.

Convergent and divergent approaches

There are two kinds of 'thinking' when solving problems. The first is analytical, or convergent, and is usually associated with left brain thinking. This approach, while rarely producing surprise eurekas, does work with straightforward problems, even complex ones, provided you can define what you want and there is a linear or logical route to a solution. Several of the methods I describe are essentially of this convergent type and you may already be familiar with them. But in each case I have added a lateral or right brain element, so some have had major adaptation, even though the names may sound familiar.

The other approach is provocative rather than analytical and looks at things from as many different viewpoints as possible, 'turning things on their head' in an attempt to get a novel insight. This is the lateral or divergent approach, using what are termed reframing techniques. In this case there are no steps that you can follow to a predictable solution. Just about all the techniques that follow fulfil this provocative requirement to stimulate right brain thinking. In practice we always use both sides of the brain, so a combination of logical and lateral problem-solving techniques, which most of these techniques comprise, often works best. So there is some analysis, but you will also have to use your imagination and think outside usual patterns.

Horses for courses

The techniques that follow vary, both in their function and characteristics. Some can be carried out in a few minutes while others require a lot longer to do them justice. Some are more akin to creativity concepts (such as reversal or chunking) which you can apply informally in just about any problem situation imaginable, while others are more systematic and focused, with rigorous ground rules to be followed to make them work well. Some were designed for group use, particularly for a business application, such as the various brainwriting methods (several of which originated in Japan), and I have included these as many readers will want to apply them in a team management situation. Most, however, can be used individually and every one can be adapted to use on your own. So this part of the book is very DIY. In the group cases, a few get best results with independent facilitation — in other words a bit of expertise. But this is more to supervise the process than add any creative input, which, after reading this book, you will be well capable of yourself. Some techniques require a specific goal or problem to start with, while others can be used to search for opportunities when you don't know what they are. Some are specifically for problem finding or defining rather than problem solving. 'Problem insight', or asking the right question, as we have already seen, often represents 90 per cent of the answer in any case, so these lateral approaches to problem definition can be powerful.

So, in choosing which technique to use, it's horses for courses. Read through the chapter first to get an idea of what is available, what best fits the sort of problems or performance outcomes you want to address and what methods appeal to you personally.

From training your brain to peak performance

How do these techniques translate into peak performance? Performance is about achieving goals or outcomes, which means changing the state you are now in and achieving another state as in Figure 2.

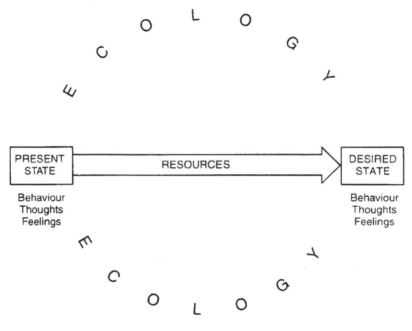

Fig 2. Change of State

Right brain intuition and creativity is also about achieving goals, as we have already seen. It does not happen in a vacuum. Every method here meets that criterion of helping you achieve outcomes. Outcomes, problems and opportunities can all be related. You can switch an outcome into problem terms. If your goal is to get to B, your problem is that you are not there — you are still at A; and, presumably, you don't know how to get there. **Problem**: How to get from A to B. Or you can switch a problem into outcome terms. **Outcome**: To solve the problem and achieve the better state you are after. So a 'problem-solving' tool can be used to help you achieve goals and capture opportunities. An 'opportunity search' tool (as some of the following techniques are) can be used to come up with creative ways to solve a problem.

However you define what you desire — solving a problem, seizing an opportunity, fulfilling a dream, achieving a target — a change of state is required. At minimum, *you* have got to change, including in how you feel (successful, happy, fulfilled). You might want to have things, know things, be able to do things, be something and feel different. Training your brain means that you will habitually achieve self-set goals, solve problems and seize opportunities. The following techniques will help you to achieve your desired performance goals. Adapt them as you want to, but give them a try at least.

Stimulating flashes and flow

How do these techniques affect the two key creative experiences which I said account for the lion's share of human excellence? Although subject to all the principles and conditions covered in the book so far, insights might well pop up while you are doing the exercises. But in most cases ideas will follow from the process of analysis and conscious thought. Logical solutions may well occur, and may be useful and satisfying — just like arriving at the answer to a maths problem — but not surprising. These are not insights. The extra exposure to the problem or goal that the technique involves, however, is likely to produce insights after an incubation period, whether of minutes, hours or days.

The flow experience also depends on the lifestyle and belief lessons you learnt in Chapter 7. These provocative techniques, however, do help you to unlearn left brain patterns of thinking or mindsets and use your unconscious, intuitive mind to create new patterns. This involves skills that require practice and form habits just like any physical skill. So persevere in acquiring the skills, just by repetition and familiarity, and leave the shortcut problem solving to your unconscious brain.

In some cases a flow experience will start while you are doing an exercise. Brainstorming groups often get into a 'high' during which ideas come in floods. On other occasions it may happen the following day or not at all — you cannot call up right brain experiences to order. But both eurekas and flow experiences respond to any concentrated exposure to your problem or outcome, just as a dream may relate to the problems of the day.

The techniques that follow are in alphabetical order so you can use them to refer to easily. Where another technique is referred to which is also included in the chapter I have used italic type so that you can again easily make cross reference.

BALLOON DIAGRAMS

These are the forerunners of mindmaps, a term coined by Tony Buzan. Other terms have been used to describe this and similar techniques so don't get confused by titles. This is a simple way to represent your thoughts in a more graphical way. Instead of making a list of ideas and thoughts from the top to the bottom of the page, you start off with the subject enclosed in an oval at the top of the page. The thoughts that stem from the subject are represented by spokes linking to other circled topics, with sub-ideas added like branches and twigs on a tree (see figure 3).

The advantage of this freewheeling technique is that it does not matter what order you put things in. You can extend a branch with further spokes as they occur to you. You can then make the diagram more useful with a little analysis, usually after you have constructed your first draft. For example the topics can be put in rectangles and diamond shapes as well as ovals to indicate different kinds of main sub-topics. A further refinement is to shade these in different ways to give a further meaning to the overall subject picture. Figure 3b is an example of a balloon diagram using these extra devices and you will see just how much information can be contained on a single sheet using this method.

Fig 3. Balloon Diagram (i)

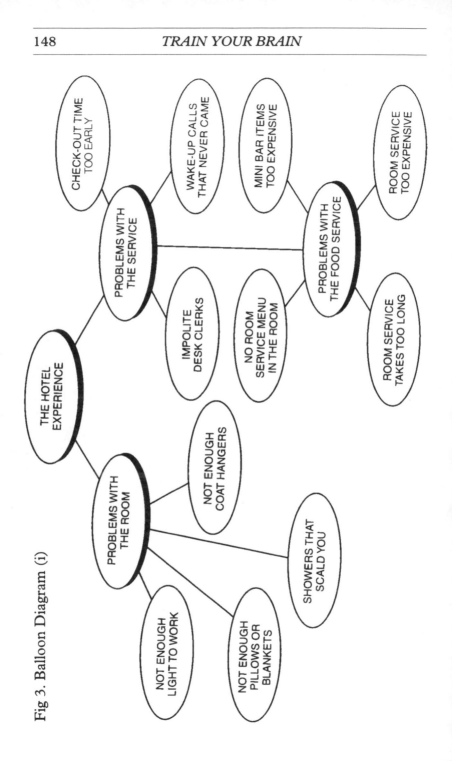

Fig 3b. Balloon Diagram (ii)

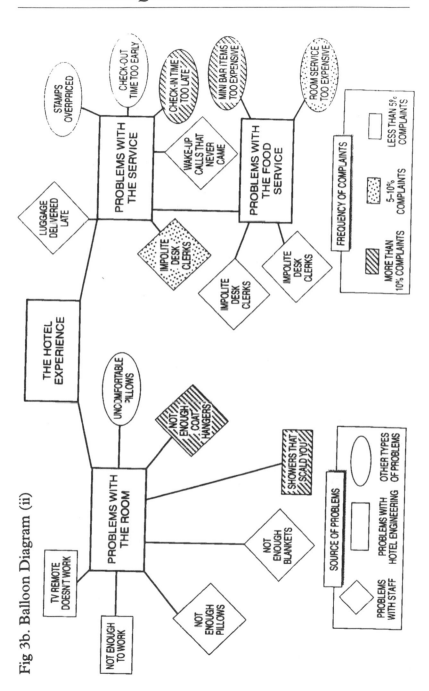

BRAINSTORMING

This method has been around for a long time and is one of the most popular creative techniques, especially when groups are involved. You need about half a dozen people and some specific problems or issues to address. The idea is to spark off as many creative ideas in as much volume as you can, regardless of whether the ideas will work, and avoiding all forms of judgement and criticism. A facilitator may be needed to keep things on track and to record ideas as they emerge.

Brainstorming ground rules

These are the basic rules that make this such a powerful group creativity tool:

1. Criticism is ruled out. Keep any judgements and evaluation until later — that is a different process.

2. Freewheeling is welcomed. The wilder the idea, the better.

3. Go for quantity. The greater the number of ideas, the greater the chance of winners.

4. Seek for combinations and improvement. That is, be ready to add to and build on other people's ideas to make them better. Or put two ideas together to make a better one.

Tests have shown that the more ideas a group generates the more good ideas result. The quality does not deteriorate with quantity. Trains of thought tend to develop and ideas synthesise so often they come out in both quantity and quality a little way into the session, which should not be long — maybe half an hour, as intense concentration and motivation is needed.

The technique has its disadvantages, however, and the main ones are to do with the group dynamics. Rarely do people in a group act without inhibition, as there may be bosses or more assertive colleagues who, quite unintentionally, suppress the ideas of others. The best ideas, moreover, may not come from the loudest people. Thus, for example, usually a brainstorming session follows the ubiquitous 80/20 rule with 80 per cent of the talking done by 20 per cent of the participants. In a typical session, one or two people will not utter a word. With in-house sessions involving an existing team, or people who are well acquainted, company politics and culture usually come into play, and some people will not feel that the organisation's culture supports them. Mistakes and risk taking may be frowned upon, for instance, and some topics held dear by management may be taboo. In fact brainstorming rarely achieves its ideal of being non-judgemental.

Many consultants and companies have abandoned the practice for this reason, especially now that so many other more effective techniques are available. As it happens, an individual in a creative frame of mind can come up with more ideas than the average per capita from a group session. The benefit of the group, however, is the wider experience base upon which ideas are drawn. *Brainwriting,* the next technique I describe, overcomes some of the disadvantages of brainstorming and other group methods. But the basic ground rules for brainstorming are useful in any creative thinking situation.

BRAINWRITING

This involves the silent, written generation of ideas in a group. All the basic brainstorming rules such as separating idea generation from evaluation and suspending judgement apply. There are several versions (brainwriting pool, KJ method, lotus blossom method, NKH brainstorming, pin cards), of which I will give two examples here.

Brainsketching

Most people use visual images to process ideas and often sketch them to help their thinking. The brainsketching technique attempts to capitalise on this ability in a group situation by allowing people to compare idea sketches.

Here are the steps:

1. Each group member individually draws a sketch of how the problem might be solved. No discussion is permitted during this stage.

2. Group members pass their drawings to the persons on their right.

3. Each person modifies the original drawings and adds comments, passing the amended drawing to the person on their right.

Everyone has a creative input, and ideas can be later clarified, expanded and synthesised to arrive at the best solution.

Brainwriting pool

In this group technique individual members, numbering say five to eight people, write down four ideas on a sheet of paper, then place their sheets in the centre of the table, exchanging it for another completed sheet. Each member then uses the ideas on the new sheet to stimulate further ideas, which are written down on the sheet. Ideas can evolve, sharing not just individual creativity but also the varied technical experience of the subject. When they need additional stimulation, they will again exchange sheets and carry on generating new ideas. As with brainstorming, a specific problem or issue is addressed. The absence of verbal exchanges avoids 'political' interference and the disadvantages of group dynamics. The sheets are a permanent record of ideas and can be revisited at any time.

CHUNKING

The idea of chunking in creative problem solving is to lift a problem or issue either to a higher level, seeing 'the big picture', or to a lower, more detailed or focused level. In practice either perspective may unblock a problem. For example a tiny detail can bog down an important negotiation in which both sides stand to gain or lose a lot, but have not identified the specific sticking points. Similarly, many problems almost disappear when we see them in a bigger context, and can get away from the detail that occupies our mind and emotions.

But the concept of chunking is wider than this and is important in creating the associations upon which insights are invariably based. To illustrate this, start with any word or idea you like. For example, I've just thought of clock. To chunk up clock I might suggest 'instrument', then chunking up further perhaps 'artefact' — increasing higher category levels. Chunking downwards I might come up with 'face' and 'hands', or any other part of the clock, or the specific clock in my study. Sideways or lateral chunking of clock would suggest perhaps watch or barometer or even ruler — different kinds of measuring instruments of which clock is an example.

Exploring any problem or issue by making upward, downward and lateral chunks can provoke associations upon which creative insights are usually based, while, unlike in the case of random ideas including *metaphors*, there is still some link with the initial idea. Lateral chunking might also be lateral in the de Bono 'lateral thinking' sense — the association might be novel, unusual or ingenious. Thus chunking down tree to beech, you could make a further downward chunk to pebble, using another meaning of 'beach'. Or a computer disk could be chunked up to spine, again using 'disk' in a different context. Often the mental associations that result in surprising eurekas are far from logical — and if so only with hindsight. Or they may be subjective, making sense only to the person involved.

Using this idea for problem solving can be very productive. Let's say that as a manager you have to discipline a member of staff who has not been pulling their weight or perhaps has been unpunctual. This is causing you difficulties, both in how you feel about the task and also in needing to know just how to do it and the words to use. Upward chunking might see the issue as one of interpersonal communication, expressing yourself clearly and honestly, relationships (not wanting to upset a colleague or lose a friend) and courage (to face up to difficult tasks). Any of these might be closer to the real problem than the specific problem task in question. Moreover, the different perspective might change the nature and importance of the matter.

For example you can probably think of occasions when you had to have courage and do some unpleasant duty, but have lived to tell the story and are no worse off for it. The new perspective will affect how you feel about the task. Or, in the matter of relationships you might ponder the fact that the best relationships are based on mutual honesty. Or that interpersonal communication comes down to skills and practice and, not surprisingly, we don't get too much practice at certain jobs. So you are not so hard on yourself. But you can at least practise mentally until you have the confidence you need and are happy about how you will do the job.

Chunking the same problem downwards might give other perspectives. Is it this particular person that is the trouble, rather than the job of disciplining staff generally? Is it the nature of the inefficiency (say timekeeping) and how this affects the work and your own performance, or simply the relationship with the individual (whatever the nature of the unsatisfactory performance). That is, what part might be the crux of the problem? Would it be different if you were to do it in writing rather than face to face, informally rather than formally (say after work)?

Sideways chunking might introduce other examples of 'straight talking' which puts this task in a different light and takes the heat out of the situation — for example if your children, a salesperson or supplier, or member of the tennis team are the object of the discipline. It may be that the context throws you and that you actually have all the skill needed to do the job. A new mental perspective may be all that is needed or a simple analogy. By chunking upwards, downwards and laterally these reframes are explored and a creative breakthrough is likely. This is also one of the several perspectives in the *sleight of mouth* technique.

Chunked reversal

This is a combination of the *reversal* and *chunking* techniques. You not only turn the problem or issue on its head by the reversal, but you capitalise on it by exploring the many perspectives and issues that chunking opens up. Figure 4, on the next page, is an example of a chunked reversal. 'Less fattening centre' is the breakthrough marketing concept.

THE CONCEPT FAN

The idea in this case is to work a problem backwards to try to get at root problems. As an example let's say your starting purpose is to be financially independent (expressed as a problem: 'I am not financially independent, but would like to be'). Working backwards a number of concepts or issues come to mind. Examples are better job, business idea, marriage partner, national lottery and so on. Your ideas will be different to mine, of course. Each of these might lead on to or 'feed' your purpose. Going further backwards, these concepts might in turn trigger their own ideas. In the case of 'better job', for instance, 'qualifications', 'age', 'talk to Jack', 'selling on commission', 'promotion', 'networking' and so on, might instinctively come to mind.

Each of these concepts can be taken further back still as more ideas occur. For example, the idea 'qualifications' might trigger 'correspondence course', 'new career', 'time', 'children', 'badminton', 'age' and so on. Thus a hierarchy or cascade of perceptions emerges that may produce the insight that will help bring about your purpose. This can happen at any point during the process or later after incubating the matter. Or you may decide to redefine your problem or change your purpose. Figure 5, on page 157, illustrates a concept fan.

Statement and chunking	reversal	issue	so?
Chocolates are bad for you	Chocolates are good for you	They are both good and bad - but it's how people perceive them.	Can we make ours seem less bad and more good? Are our chocolates just like others?
Chocolates make you fat.	Chocolates do not make you fat	There are bits that do and bits that don't. It's the feeling of guilt - our perception . . .	Can we reduce the guilt a bit?
Maltychocs make you fat	Maltychocs do not make you fat	What if they didn't? Can't we make this an opportunity?	Can we change the image, the packaging. . .?
Parts of Maltychocs make you fat	Parts of Maltychocs do not make you fat	What parts? The filling? Can we change anything?	What strengths can we work on? Can we capitalise on the fatness thing?
The chocolate coat is the problem	The chocolate is not the problem	So should we concentrate on the filling	We can't do much about the chocolate. The centre isn't that fattening . . . it's *less fattening* than most of the competition.

Fig 4. Chunked reversal

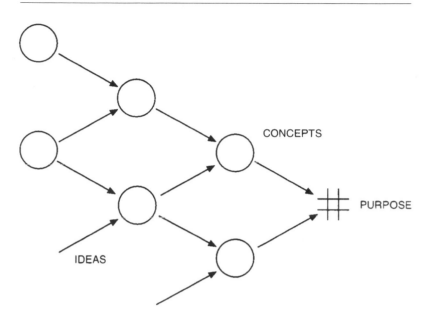

Fig 5. The Concept Fan

At each stage backwards the ideas tend to be more practical in nature and less conceptual. So, for example, the longer term and rather general goal of financial independence might bring you right back to a specific activity or decision; making a telephone call for night school course details, having a chat with one of your children to see what they think about you spending time studying or deciding finally to hang up the badminton racquet. So perceptions, however conceptually broad, can be translated into action that will affect your external reality and future.

By adopting an intuitive method such as this, and this means letting your thoughts flow spontaneously rather than in a logical, careful way, any one of the triggers in the exercise might be surprising ('That may be interesting', 'I had never thought of that before', 'That puts a different light on things'). As well as the pleasure in the process the surprise element is a feature of creative thinking methods like this. This technique is very similar to the *flowscape*.

DYNAMIC SWOTS

The SWOT analysis (strengths, weaknesses, opportunities, threats) is a well-proven technique you have probably used before. It is especially powerful when considering strategic issues, at a business unit or corporate level, but can also be applied at a personal level, such as when considering a job or career change.

This is a classical analytical tool, of course. But a major adaptation is to make the tool dynamic so that you can address SWOT 'values' over a period and as between different business units, or companies within a group. Here is how to do it.

First list your SWOT factors as normal. Remember that typically strengths and weaknesses will be internal to the company or business unit, and opportunities and threats tend to be external. For present purposes try to get a similar number — say half a dozen — in each of the four categories, so that you are obliged to think further if you have tended to ignore, say, your weaknesses or threats, and have a cut off when you are inclined to multiply your strengths (or for that matter your weaknesses), if that is the tradition or management culture in your organisation. Some managers seem unable to spot anything wrong with their company and others cannot see anything right.

Next *weight* each factor. This is the important subjective part of the exercise. One weakness (say 'Very high staff turnover' or 'Factory accommodation is bursting at the seams') might be equivalent to five of the others, so you need to weight it by a factor of five (X 5). Another item might be weighted by a factor of 2 (X 2). Or you might lump two factors in your list together, effectively giving them the value of a half each.

Now construct a matrix as in Figure 6. The horizontal or west-east axis represents threats and opportunities, and the vertical south-north axis represents weaknesses and strengths. By using a simple scale on each axis, then taking the net difference of the strengths and weaknesses weighted total you can plot threats and opportunities on the horizontal scale. That is, if opportunities exceed threats by say 4 you will mark the axis 4 to the right from the centre. Similarly plot the net difference of the strengths and weaknesses on the vertical axis. In the example this is towards the strengths end of the vertical axis. If threats exceed opportunities your position will finish up on the left of the matrix, and vice versa. You can then plot the result which will fall in one of the four quadrants. The north-east (top right) quadrant is where you want to be (plenty of opportunities and strengths) and within that quadrant as far to the top right-hand corner as you can get.

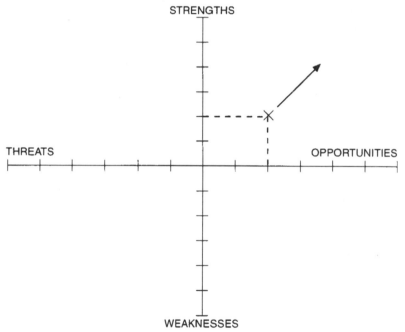

Fig 6. Dynamic Swot Matrix

If you finish up in the top left quadrant, although you have internal strengths to build upon, you need to eliminate, neutralise or insure against threats, while at the same time exploiting or creating opportunities. In other words move to the right — or east. You will also try to increase your strengths and reduce your weaknesses to move further to the top — or north. In other words, always try to move towards the north east.

If your SWOT analysis finishes up in the bottom right quadrant you need to start building on or creating internal strengths and tackling weaknesses. If you finish up in the bottom left quadrant you need to carry out all these exercises in an attempt to move up and to the right on the matrix — to the north-east.

You can have a plan or projection version of a SWOT which might relate to a one-year or five-year business plan. By redoing the dynamic SWOT from time to time you can monitor your strategic success just as in monitoring against a financial budget.

This process is, of course, largely a matter of more analysis and will not necessarily result in creative thinking. However, by seeing the picture graphically, as a whole (holistically) and also as a movement in business performance rather than a fixed picture, you are getting close to a right brain way of processing. So this process is more likely to bring the 'aha' insights that will help to move you in the right direction, both on the matrix and in business success.

What has probably already become apparent to you is:

➤ the importance of which factors you choose;

➤ the weighting of each;

➤ the need to get at root problems and make changes.

Other techniques might help. A *brainwriting* approach will produce plenty of ideas as to what goes into the first SWOT. Weighting is subjective and a quick, instinctive approach is probably better than a laboured, analytical one. If you want to get at a team weighting it is better to do the job individually, then take an average, rather than expose yourself to all the negative team dynamics and extra time any attempt at consensus usually involves. The real creativity comes when you start to decide on what to do about the situation, which is why the dynamic matrix is such a good starting tool.

FLOWSCAPES

This is one way to get your ideas into a graphical form which often brings with it new insights. Flowscapes introduce some structure and attempt to mirror what actually happens in the mind. It is a very practical tool you can use either for problem solving or getting insights into any subject. It is based on the idea that thoughts flow one to another, rather like the party game where you say the first thing that comes to your mind on hearing a word, or the random association techniques that psychiatrists use. In this sense perception is very dynamic and thought patterns 'flow' continuously. In terms of lateral thinking, for any thought or idea, we are not so much concerned with *what this is* as with *where might this lead;* not with reinforcing existing mindsets, but with creating new, more useful ones. I will first describe the process then give a simple example that will make it clear.

➤ Decide on your subject — the problem, issue or opportunity you want to explore.

➤ Write down the things that come into your mind as you think about it, using a couple of words or very short phrases (stream of consciousness list).

➤ Aim for at least half a dozen thoughts but no more than twenty.

➤ Give each perception you list a letter A, B, C and so on.

➤ When your 'base list' is complete, and you cannot think of any other aspects of the subject, decide which of the other thoughts in your list naturally follows or flows from the one you are considering — where the thought you are considering might lead.

➤ Arrange your list graphically with an arrow going from each letter to one other letter so that every one is accounted for

(A, B, C, D right to the last one) but once only, and every one is linked to one of the others in the list.

➤ The perception you flow to can be used as many times as you like (so A, B and C, for example, may all lead to F).

Your list of thoughts can be in any order, but when you come to draw the flowscape you may need to do a draft first, so that the finished result is neat enough for you to make sense of. I will use one of the examples from Edward de Bono's book *Water Logic*, so that if you want to learn more about the technique you can carry on with the more detailed examples he gives, besides learning more background about the theory of water logic on which the technique is based. Your own flowscape will not need such a long description, and usually one or two words will suffice both for the subject (for example, 'Difficult boss', 'Helen's tantrums', 'Overdraft frozen') and also the listed thoughts ('Need reference', 'Has family problems', 'Good at his job', 'Not for ever').

Subject

You have a faithful and loyal manager who has worked hard for you over the years. He is getting older and the work is getting too much for him. He has not yet reached retirement age and he is unwilling to take early retirement.

List

The letters on the right are what the perceptions on the list 'lead to'.

A	Been with you many years and loyal	I
B	Does not want to retire	E
C	There is a need for a new person	F
D	Money is no problem	B
E	Turf and territory is a problem	B
F	Difficult to indicate inadequacy	G

G	Manager is a sensitive person	I
H	It has to happen some time	C
I	Effect on morale elsewhere	B
J	Hints have been ignored and rejected	B

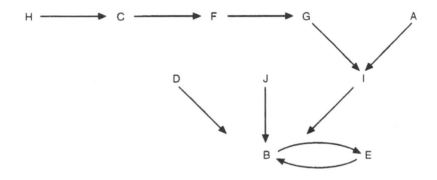

Fig 7. Flowscape

Note there is no right and wrong, either in the thoughts you list or where you decide they flow to. The flowscape is about your perceptions, which is what most problems boil down to, rather than external reality. Your list may not make sense to another person. You may miss out items your colleague thinks should be there and include others he might think are nothing to do with the subject. Even more, he may not understand why one issue for you would follow another. It is *your* flowscape that will help you get an overall picture by widening your perception of the matter. When you come to do an actual flowscape you will see how quickly you can gain insights into how you are approaching the problem and what are the important aspects, and be able to make a better quality decision.

Now let's examine the example flowscape shown in Figure 7.

Point B   This is termed a collector point, because several items lead into it. The manager simply does not want to retire. To sack him would be both ungrateful for his loyal services and would affect morale elsewhere.

Point I   This is also a collector point which collects up some other feeders and then feeds them into B. In essence, it affirms that sacking is not an option.

Chain H-C-F-G   The need for a change indicated by this chain is eventually blocked by the impossibility of retiring the manager against his will.

Loop B-E   This is known as a stable loop. Comprising just two elements of the list, it is a very simple one. Quite simply, the manager does not want to retire and does not want to give up his territory or turf. So there is no possibility of moving him to a different position. The solution might be to promote him and to have other people working under him. This way he gets to keep the turf but the work he cannot cope with gets done by other people.

The flowscape also indicates that working on points D and J is not going to make much difference.

As we have already seen, we process thoughts in patterns, that become stronger and stronger as our experience reinforces them. In the flowscape these are represented by collector points or stable loops. Obviously if you can solve a collector point issue all the subsidiary issues on your list are taken care of. A stable loop, of which every flowscape will have at least one (try it out, and check in de Bono's book if you want to learn the theory behind it), represents a stable, well-entrenched perception. This usually confirms what is well understood, accepted, obvious or at least perceived to be so. The perception, however, may or may not truly reflect external reality (i.e. you may have read the situation wrongly, however entrenched your perception).

Dealing only in perceptions, including intuitions, the flowscape is not an analytical tool. If you were to logically analyse the situation you might have written out a different list. Conversely, you might miss spontaneous ideas and feelings which are crucial to a solution. A perception might be to do with how you feel about the subject, for instance, or a thought that just enters your mind as you write down your list, even though you are not sure why. Neither of these is the sort of thought that would appear in an analysis that may have to be supported or argued logically, although it may well be significant to you and help with a decision. Similarly, in this case you would not link up with what elements lead to, as logic is about what is rather than what it might lead to.

FORCE FIELD ANALYSIS

This method identifies the positive and negative factors or forces working for and against your goal or within a problem. Like a SWOT analysis, this is an analytical tool, so we will have to apply some lateral thinking.

Let's say that the problem is that since John took over the northern region the results have slipped badly. The chances are that although you want better results you don't want to sack John, spend the time bringing another sales manager up to scratch, living with an even worse performance in the interim and so on. So there are conflicting issues. If you were to decide what you really want, which is presumably good company results with a contented workforce, you could identify forces working for and against that outcome. For example, positive forces might be your historical market domination, good technical people and a wide distribution base. Negative forces might be increasing competition, some new technology that your main competitor has adopted and of course John's poor performance. The problem exists because there is a conflict between these positive and negative forces. There is a stalemate and the idea is to upset the equilibrium that the problem represents (Figure 8).

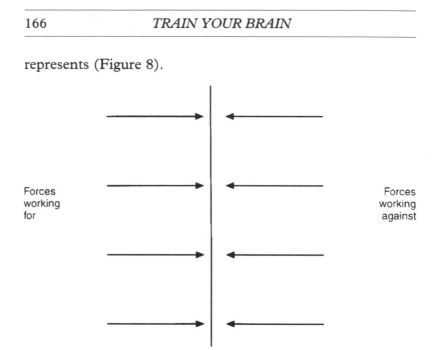

Fig 8. Force-field Analysis

If there are no downsides to firing John you don't have a problem — the decision is straightforward and you just have to do it. If you didn't have to keep earning profits and paying out dividends the competition would not be a problem nor the changing technology. It's the conflict that makes the problem. So this kind of analysis makes sense.

However, the weakness is that usually the positive and negative forces are well known and each person in an organisation (especially at the same level) tends to come up with the same analysis and recommendations, but without the core problem being solved. Any manager worth his or her salt will be well aware of the pros and cons and all the standard company wisdom. Even a competitor could do a reasonable force field analysis on what they also know to be your key problems. What is needed is a breakthrough, which by its very nature has to be creative and surprising rather than obvious or the sequential result of a logical process.

There are three types of force field:

➤ 'A versus B' which defines two conflicting goals or outcomes. In effect on one side of a sheet of paper you identify what you want and on the other side you put what you don't want. You should be able to treat or 'label' any problem in this way, restating it in terms of what you would rather the situation was.

➤ The second type of force field is the 'obstacles' kind. In this format you list what you want or what you need and on the other side what prevents you from getting it. Again this deals in goals or outcomes.

➤ In the third type, having identified what you want, you list the forces that are helping you to achieve it and on the other side those forces that are preventing you from getting what you want. In this case the technique is taken to a lower level of analysis and might apply to the outcomes in either of the first two types of force field.

Here is an example of the third type:

What do I want? _____

Things helping me

_____
_____
_____
_____

Things preventing me

_____
_____
_____
_____

Fig 9. Force-field Analysis (ii)

These are powerful techniques but you can make them far more creative and effective by drawing on other techniques. As I said at the start, conventional analytical techniques can be made far more creative and effective by adaptation, including force field analysis. Try the following alternatives:

1. Reverse every positive or negative statement you make (see how to do this in the *reversal* technique). This will upset company or personal mindsets that tend to be accepted rather than challenged.

2. Select any interesting ideas that come from this exercise and apply further lateral techniques, such as *brainstorming, brainwriting,* or *sleight of mouth.* This might turn a negative force into a positive one, eliminate or weaken an apparent negative force, or make a positive force stronger.

3. Do the analysis from the point of view of a specific major competitor, supplier or customer/client. Imagine they were doing the exercise in respect of your firm (which as a smart competitor they might well do) and what their thinking would be. Give careful consideration to any differences from your 'own' version.

4. Rank the factors you have chosen in order of importance, then consider them in reverse — that is, assuming that the least important factor is the most important one. This again will upset entrenched thinking.

5. Try *metaphors and analogies.*

6. Take your negative forces as symptoms and use the *root cause* technique to get back to the core or root problem.

7. Try applying the *'how to' diagram* to negative forces.

8. Use visualisation. See the situation as you would like it to be. Do not spare any detail, but observe everything about the new created future; listen to what people say, notice the reaction of competitors, staff, your boss etc.

'HOW TO' DIAGRAM

This is a device for redefining your problem creatively. It focuses on the fact that to solve a problem you usually have to do something, not just think of theoretical answers. It is highly practical in asking how to, rather than why or even what to do. It is similar to some other techniques in attempting to get back to the source of your problem which, as we have seen, usually turns out to be quite different from the one you started with, or were presented with, and also more simple.

As an example let's say the problem is that you have received a particularly big telephone bill and you are not sure how you will manage to pay it along with all your other expenses. Start by restating your problem prefixed by 'how to'. In this case, 'How to pay the telephone bill'. Then think of any other 'how to' that might better define the problem you have or, as you saw in the *concept fan* technique, gets to what might be the root to the problem — for example, 'how to' (abbreviated to HT) use the phone less'. Your mind is now switched to the usage of the phone and the obvious question of who is running up the big bills. 'HT keep Laura [your teenage daughter] off the phone' may thus be your next instinctive 'how to'. Then, perhaps, 'HT be straight with her'; 'HT be consistent' (you give in so many times on this and other matters); 'HT say no to Laura'. Don't stop until you have gone as far back as you can. You might finish up with 'HT say no' — not just to Laura about using the phone, but in many other situations in your life. In this case the problem turns out to be a big one, certainly not confined to unpaid bills, but at least you have got to the bottom of it. If seriously addressed the chances are that lots of other problems, involving relationships and work matters, as well as big telephone bills, will be solved into the bargain. It's always best to know the real, underlying problem, which this technique will help you to identify. The solution is then not such a big issue, usually both simple and effective. The problem, it turns out, is not just about paying the telephone bill, but nor is it intractable.

In practice your telephone bill 'how to's' might have gone very differently. For example, you might have pursued 'HT get a bank overdraft' or 'HT economise in other areas'. Then, you might look at 'HT pay off the overdraft. HT earn more money. HT get more overtime at work. HT get a better job', and so on. Often each different avenue you take brings you back to the same root problem, much like the loop in the *flowscape* technique. In other cases you may finish up with several problems. But it's better to know you have such problems than to carry on ignorantly and probably make things worse. In the above case, it is very useful self-knowledge that you have difficulty saying no to people and that this gets you into all kinds of trouble — including big telephone bills. The revelation may come as a surprise, as a creative insight about yourself. Or it may confirm what you knew all along but would not have associated with the telephone bill problem. Either way the *'how to' technique* is a powerful way of achieving top performance. Give it a try. It can be applied to all kinds of work and personal situations.

I prefer to use this technique in the form of a diagram much like *balloon diagrams* and *mindmaps*. I start in the middle and extend the how to's outwards as spokes, using a different spoke for each line of thinking. You can then see the lines of thinking that turn out to be culs-de-sac and those that are more enlightening. As with other creativity techniques, an insight, be it a solution, a pertinent question or better definition of your problem, can occur at any stage in the process, or after incubating the matter. Figure 10 shows the telephone bill example in this graphical format, but using a familiar hierarchy or tree rather than spokes from a central hub.

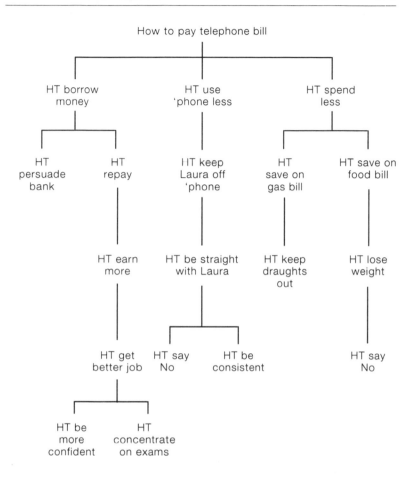

Fig 10. How-to Diagram

METAPHORS AND ANALOGIES

Similar results can be achieved by using metaphors and analogies. We employ these all the time in thinking but rarely use them in a positive way for problem solving.

The manufacturing process for lead shot was based on the analogy of falling raindrops that take on a spherical character. A 'shot tower' was used to drop the molten lead into water-filled vats. But that wasn't all. Those that were not spherical were removed using the simple analogy that spheres roll down a slight incline, while the misshapen shot did not. Orville and Wilbur Wright used the condor, a soaring bird, as the model they were trying to emulate in their flying machine. Being in the bicycle business, they also realised by analogy that they would have to learn how to fly their aircraft as well as build it.

Charles Babbage almost built the first computer in 1833. Having already perfected a complicated control system for weaving machines, using punched cards threaded together, he decided that his new machine could weave numbers in the same way that a loom could weave flowers and leaves. Radar was modelled on the echo-ranging system that flying bats use to navigate. Edison, as well as inventing the incandescent light bulb, also invented city-wide electrical systems in which dynamos were linked by branching power lines to thousands of lamps. His remarkable analogy was the maple tree in his back garden. 'Nature doesn't just make leaves', he observed, 'it makes branches and trees and roots to go with them'.

Metaphors can be from nature — such as trees, clouds, a hedgehog, an albatross, the moon, roses, sunrise etc. Or you can choose man-made metaphors — a suspension bridge, a coal mine, a toothbrush, a garden pond or whatever. 'Sheila is a brick' or 'John is a treasure' are examples of metaphors used as mental pictures or associations that help us to know Sheila and John better.

In the same way metaphors can help throw light on any real

situation, issue or problem. In using metaphor as a creative technique you need not stick to clichéd metaphors like those above. Indeed the characteristics you draw out and associations you make might never have been made before — by you or anyone else. So there is room for originality, surprises and insights. And while you might not score with an answer every time, unlike a mathematical problem or computer program, when you do the originality and novelty will usually be far beyond what a logical process could ever produce. For real problems (rather than pretend problems — puzzles — with a single right answer), creative thinking through associating metaphors is simply more effective.

Metaphors and analogies can be in the form of processes rather than things — for example boiling an egg, climbing a mountain, hibernation, learning to type, making a daisy chain, building a tower block, a tree growing or whatever. These fulfil the same provocative function and can trigger associations with the problem or matter in hand. It is upon such unusual associations that insights are usually based.

The effect is similar with random words where the association with a trigger word might be tenuous and subjective, yet none the less meaningful to the person thinking of it. You may find, however, that natural metaphors and analogies (besides being in abundant supply) are the most powerful, and it is the case that many great inventions have been inspired by the fantastic world of nature. Well-known stories and fables can be also useful, as can proverbs and sayings. These do not have to be carefully matched with the problem. That happens in the mind of the problem holder as unconscious creative associations produce their own 'aha' revelations.

Where do you get your metaphors and analogies from? Anywhere. Look out of your window. Turn on the television. Flick through a magazine and choose a picture or topic at random. Close your eyes and take whatever comes into your mind. The metaphor does not have to be closely related to the problem. Some aspect of the analogy might be linked to the problem or vice versa, and this catches your attention, but this is not important. The idea is to break up rather than prop up outdated mental patterns and provoke or tease out associations that would not have occurred to you in a logical consideration of the problem. The effort of relating the analogy forces you to look at things in a new way and this is what brings the insight. As examples, here are some problems/situations, and suggested analogies and metaphors.

Getting your work up to date so that you can take a few days' holiday

➤ A willow tree

➤ A combine harvester

➤ A photocopier

➤ Doing a driving test

➤ Cutting the lawn

Low staff morale

➤ Snowballs

➤ A waterfall

➤ Keeping bees

➤ Driving a steam engine

Keeping your desk tidy

➤ Pyramids

➤ Nouvelle cuisine

➤ Felling trees

➤ Saving up for your holiday

➤ Sailing round the world

➤ Doing the weekly shopping

Have a go at these for practice. Use the relaxation method and other suggestions in Chapter 7 to get into the right frame of mind. If you have difficulty move to another one and you might find that ideas come to your mind. The process is usually one of moving repeatedly between the analogy and the problem. One aspect of the analogy might associate with tidying your desk (like, in the case of 'weekly shopping', having a list, being regular and disciplined, choosing the best time, the fact that you can't get out of it, the benefits, the interesting aspects, using skills — like guessing how much the bill will come to, and so on). Usually more connections are made and ideas begin to flow.

In effect the problem moves on with the analogy and the analogy moves on with the problem. Each may be developed, explored or expanded. Some aspects of the analogy (like, in the case of shopping, 'I hate it') might 'click' with the problem, and raise interesting questions, such as 'How do I manage to do the regular shopping when I hate it, yet don't keep my desk tidy?' The answer might give you insights into your desk habits. Conversely, an aspect of the problem (such as 'I don't really mind the clutter') might connect with the analogy ('I don't mind missing the shopping'). This raises the issues of the consequences (What if you did?), long and short-term implications, benefits of regular shopping, the part you least hate etc. This line of thinking might produce ingenious shortcuts you (or a friend) have devised in the analogy (like doing it very quickly and treating yourself to a snack afterwards) which might have an application to the problem.

By starting on simple cases like these in a relaxed, non-threatening mode ('It's not a big problem, so who cares, I'll just enjoy the process'), you will gain experience and confidence. Specifically, you will learn to trust your ability to come up with associations using any metaphor or analogy, and you will probably find this to be both challenging and enjoyable. Then, when you apply the technique to a real problem, you will not be so inclined to block the process with left brain criticism and analysis. Because your subconscious mind has a real outcome to pursue for your benefit, you are likely to find your ideas more creative and insightful, given experience and confidence in the process. Remember also that 'right brain' skill training in one area, such as these association type techniques, will give benefits in another, such as reframing. As well as learning how to solve problems creatively you will learn through analogy how to control how you feel. Remember also that if you do not get an answer, you might at least define your problem better or come up with a better question. Nothing you have done will be wasted, but will be handed over to the unconscious mind for its clever incubating job. Keep one or two metaphors loosely in your mind, along with the problem you are tackling and expect some ideas tomorrow morning or whenever. Be ready to revisit your problem having slept on it for a reasonable time and to repeat the process, using perhaps a different analogy or exploring the original one further. You can do this while in the shower, walking down the road or waiting for a meeting to start at work. While you are doing it the answer to an entirely different question (you were thinking about it a lot last weekend but it had gone right out of your mind) might pop into your mind. Accept it, enjoy it, and expect more as your performance gets better and better.

MINDMAPS

Mindmaps are graphical mind pictures that do a similar job to the *balloon diagram*. In this case the circled subject is in the middle, with spokes and branches extending outwards in all directions to cover as much detail as you want to on a single page. In this case you don't need to circle the sub-topics but can label the spokes themselves. It sometimes helps to use simple pictures in place of words, as long as you know what they mean, as often a simple icon or picture saves a lot of words. Working in images rather than words may well stimulate your right brain too, which will result in more creativity. You can then connect by lines thoughts that are related.

As with *balloon diagrams* you can weight your ideas by using thicker lines for the main branches. The mindmap mirrors how you think, including the way subjects are related, and the importance of these relationships. Figure 11 is an example of a mindmap. I have used the subject 'Right Brain Manager', illustrating how I used the process to plan my book of that title.

This tool can be used in different ways. It could be used as an analysis, for instance, but simply displayed in a different way, like the *balloon diagram*. This might make it easier for you to remember things and might appeal to people who are visually inclined. Or you could use it as a 'stream of consciousness' type process to generate as many ideas as possible.

The advantage of a mindmap is that instead of just having a list (like the base list for the *flowscape*) you can develop ideas down each branch as they occur to you, so there is an instant grouping of main and sub-topics and a built-in weighting of topics, as some will have lots of branches and twigs. You can see at a glance what are the major aspects of your subject. After-thoughts can easily be squeezed in and the mindmap acts as a good draft for a report or more formal document that then has to be written in ordinary narrative. All you need to do is number each spoke in the order you will cover them in your document, having given it thought. Or you can combine some of the branches to get a simpler structure. Otherwise, you may wish to produce another version of the mindmap, perhaps changing the order of the branches so that they follow clockwise in the order you finally decide upon.

As with any technique, the danger is that it can become just another analytical device which reinforces rather than questions existing mindsets, albeit in a different, visual format. So use this technique when you are in a creative mode. Nothing can replace your innate creativity. Carry out the mapping quickly and spontaneously without worrying about what relates to what or whether there will be room for new thoughts. Use a large sheet of paper or flip chart if you find this more helpful, and be ready to experiment with colours, which often foster creativity. Any technique should be a servant rather than a master. Make sure you enjoy it.

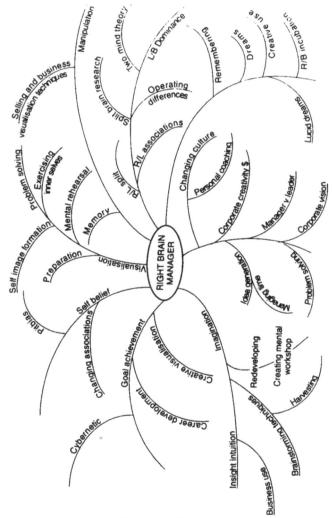

Fig 11. Mindmap

REPETITIVE WHY ANALYSIS

Extensive analysis often reveals lots of potential causes but no clear 'aha' regarding the root problem. Repetitive why analysis helps to track down the evolution of the problem. The process is like peeling an onion or revealing successive layers of paper in a package, and is illustrated in Figure 12.

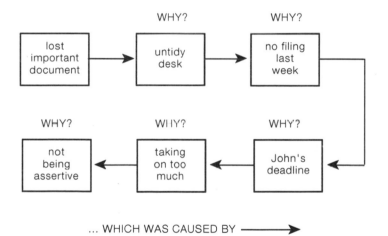

Fig 12. Repetitive Why Analysis

Start by stating the problem as clearly as you can, adding 'which was caused by ...' and enter the answer on the next line, repeating the process until you arrive at what seems like the root problem. In effect you keep asking 'why?'. Rather than use a conventional worksheet or list you may prefer to work more loosely in the style of a *balloon diagram* or *mindmap*.

Here is a simple example to illustrate how you can apply it to just about any problem:

Problem: Lost important document.
which was caused by: untidy desk
which was caused by: not filing things straight away last week
which was caused by: completing project for John's deadline
which was caused by: taking on too much work
which was caused by: not being assertive

'Not being assertive' might well be an important root cause of a lost document, or several lost documents, and indeed lots of other problems. The process could have continued very differently, of course, resulting in a root cause:

➤ you are not organised;

➤ the filing system is no use;

➤ you do not plan ahead;

➤ it was misfiled;

➤ your secretary has been away;

➤ you did not make a backup;

➤ your migraine is getting worse;

➤ you have been worried about things at home.

Note that although the nature of each root problem is very different — from a specific situation when your secretary was away to a more fundamental problem like your poor organisation skills or an inefficient filing system — the problem is at least clear and much more simple. You have a pretty good idea what needs to be done, whether the problem is a big one or a little one, and the extent to which it is in your power to resolve it.

REVERSAL

This creative concept takes the idea of different perspectives as far as possible, by completely reversing a problem statement, element or 'truth'. Rather than changing your perspective a few degrees, you do a 180 degrees turnaround. 'I don't have enough money' might become 'I've got too much money'. 'Market share is decreasing' might become 'Market share is increasing'. The new 'truth' , rather than the old one, is then addressed creatively.

The power of any creative technique is in stimulating your innate creativity which no technique can replace. In this case it just forces it harder, so even more creativity is needed to make sense of the absurdity of a reversed truth. In fact, of course, the absurdity may well be due to our perception, locked in as we are to mental patterns or mindsets. Once these mental patterns are disturbed and we are free to contemplate new possibilities — new realities if you like — then the resulting idea might not seem so absurd, but positive and sensible, at least with the benefit of hindsight. That is a characteristic of creative insights, which all these techniques try to stimulate.

There are no rules in making the reversal. You might go the full 180 degrees, making a literal reversal of the meaning as in the above examples. Or you can go a long way towards that, changing the subject, verb or object in a problem statement. For example: 'How to persuade employees to arrive on time' might be reversed to 'How to dissuade employees from turning up on time', 'How to persuade them to turn up late' or 'How to persuade them not to turn up at all'.

As with classical *brainstorming*, there is no place at all for judgement or evaluation in this process. It is the ideas arising from a reversal that produce the insights and workable solutions. For example, persuading employees to turn up late might open up the various possibilities of flexitime or basing compensation on results rather than time spent. Persuading them not to turn up at all might introduce ideas about home working, spending more time with clients, submitting their morning sales report by computer link or dismissal for chronic tardiness. Once a new line of thinking emerges, the reversal has done its job.

This is a powerful technique that has been used at the highest strategic level in companies, such as in the ubiquitous 'What business are we in?' question. To illustrate this in seminars I quote examples that executives from any industry can relate to. Using the pen business, for example, Bic pens might make the corporate statement (truth) 'We make pens'. The reversal 'We do not make pens (or we make non-pens)' raises the immediate question 'What, then, do we make?' Answer: 'Plastic things that are so cheap you don't mind losing them or throwing them away'. And this opens up the whole market of mass produced plastic extrusion products such as cups, razors, cutlery and, before long, electronic calculators.

Parker pens might make the corporate statement 'We make prestige pens', and a reversal would beg the same sort of strategic 'what business' questions as Bic. The insightful answer might be 'We make quality gifts'. Regardless of the product opportunities that such a strategic rethink offers, the competition is now not Sheaffer pens, or Waterman pens, but Remington shavers, leather briefcases or expensive perfume. Reversing 'We make pencils' might progress to a 'We make writing instruments' definition, thus avoiding dependence on a dying product by a narrow, short-sighted definition of the business. The often-quoted but no less remarkable marketing example 'Our customers don't want quarter-inch drills, they want quarter-inch holes' also illustrates the sheer power of creative as against analytical and research-based methods.

These examples underline the need for creativity all the time, rather than just when the crisis hits you, as by then some competitor has already done the insightful thinking and you are out of business.

Assumption reversal

This is an application of the reversal concept. How you treat any issue will depend on the assumptions you make about it. Creative questioning of these assumptions often produces a problem redefinition and clues about the crux of the issue or the root problem. Assumption reversal has been used when what are termed logical paradoxes are involved. For example, you need to reduce costs by 20 per cent but at the same time increase output. Or you have to sell more but with fewer people. To overcome the paradox you could reverse any problem assumptions and use the new assumptions to generate ideas.

As an example, starting with the need to improve a refrigerator, first write down all major problem assumptions:

➤ 'A refrigerator keeps food cold.'

➤ 'Opening the door lets out cold air.'

➤ 'A refrigerator requires electricity to run it.'

➤ 'A refrigerator is capable of freezing some foods.'

And so on. Reversing these assumptions (and there are no rules in how you 'reverse') you might come up with:

➤ 'A refrigerator heats food' (idea, what about a built-in microwave oven, combining the two functions).

➤ 'Opening the door helps retain cold air inside' (idea, opening the door triggers a boost of extra cold air until it is closed again).

➤ 'A refrigerator requires no electricity' (idea, a battery powered backup in the event of a power failure).

➤ 'Frozen foods always melt in a freezer' (idea, install a timed, automatic defroster).

Changing assumptions is almost certain to change the nature of the problem and your perspective on it. It is one way to creatively unblock what is an intractable situation.

ROOT CAUSE CHECKLIST

There is no sure way of knowing that you have reached the root cause of a problem. A good indication is the surprise element that accompanies any insight or 'aha' revelation — usually it is something so simple that you wonder why you had not thought of it before. For people familiar with intuitive feelings this will be a reliable indicator. In other cases you may want to apply more logical or analytical tests to what a technique has thrown up as being a possible root problem. Using a *root cause checklist* you can ask questions which together will give a good indication of whether you have got to the root or original cause of the problem.

Here are some test questions:

1. You ran into a dead end when asking the question, 'What caused the proposed root cause?'

2. All conversation on the issue has come to a positive end.

3. Everyone involved feels good, is motivated and uplifted emotionally.

4. All agree it is the root cause that keeps the present problem from resolution.

5. The root cause fully explains why the present problem exists from all points of view.

6. The earlier beginnings of the problem have been explored and understood.

7. The root cause is logical, makes sense and dispels confusion.

8. The root cause is something you can influence, control and deal with realistically.

9. Finding the root cause has returned hope that something constructive can be done about the situation.

10. Suddenly workable solutions, not outrageous demands, that deal with all the symptoms begin to appear.

11. A stable, long-term, once and for all resolution of the situation now appears feasible.

Just answer each question yes or no instinctively. A preponderance of yes answers probably means you have got at the root of the problem and can direct your effort to its solution with confidence.

SLEIGHT OF MOUTH

This is a powerful reframing technique from NLP which bridges the gap between creative freewheeling thinking, and the need for some focus and structure. With *brainstorming*, for instance, the process might get bogged down or degenerate because of a lack of structure. Some of the dozen or so 'points of view' will be familiar, such as seeing the 'big picture' or 'bird's eye view', imagining positive outcomes, or the worst that might happen. The illustration in Figure 13 shows the technique, applying it to the common problem 'There is too much work to handle'.

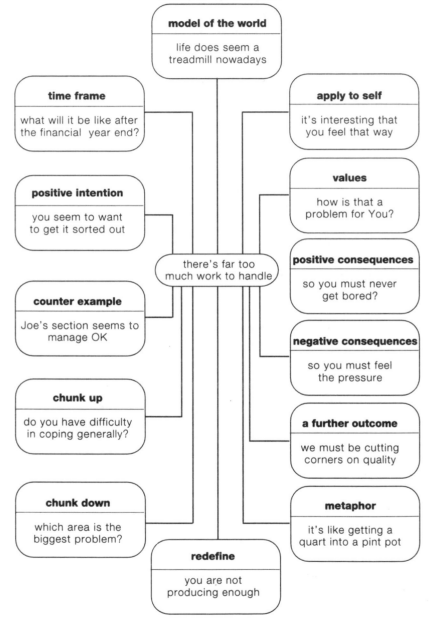

Fig 13. Sleight of Mouth

Note that each perspective might produce a number of creative insights — for example several positive outcomes, different redefinitions or any number of *metaphors*. So the process will produce scores of angles on any problem or issue, only one of which may be necessary to provide the necessary 'aha' to unblock it. You will notice the terms chunking up and chunking down, which are covered in some detail under *chunking* which is a powerful creativity method in its own right. Similarly, the metaphor point of view is covered under *metaphors and analogies*.

Any problem-solving technique will help you to think more about the issues and to focus on the matter. But there is a danger of being over-analytical, so I have emphasised the role of your own creativity in applying any such techniques. Fortunately there is no either/or decision and just about any problem will lend itself both to analysis and creative insight. Training in analytical techniques is well established and whole business schools and educational systems major on this left brain mode of thinking. As far as creativity is concerned — and in particular the eureka and flow experiences on which I have concentrated in this book — there has been a tendency to discount or ridicule such a mystical unscientific approach. And even when the evidence for its effectiveness is overwhelming the argument that creativity and insight is not trainable has the same net effect of underutilising a massive part of our brainpower. You cannot train in a logical or left brain way to have more ideas and flow experiences — the right brain holistic way is very different. But you can certainly train yourself to be open to the unconscious operations of your brain, to follow the sort of lifestyle and have the knowledge and beliefs that support and foster creativity. More than anything your brain is a fantastic learning machine and you can train it to do whatever you want it to do.

Every year of research into the human mind displays more of its complexity and potential and, like the outside universe which it so uncannily mirrors, offers no hint of a boundary. And more and more very ordinary people are learning to tap the awesome brain power in their ownership and — I hope after reading and acting on this book — control. The present knowledge revolution that is likely to produce so many self-made millionaires can now produce self-made geniuses. Or, at least — if that term still carries too much genetic baggage and mystique — people who achieve what they are capable of achieving in every aspect of their lives and enjoy the process. Start to trust and train your brain to become such a person.

9

THREE-WEEK PEAK PERFORMANCE PLAN

Most approaches to self-improvement, like getting fit, involve some form of nasty tasting medicine or unpleasant diet. Better performance usually involves perseverance against all the odds, an iron will power and a degree of self analysis that creates more guilt than productivity. Just waiting for that winning eureka, without effort, sounds incredible and far too easy. There is no pain. So it sounds too good to be true. I hope that, having read the book, your understanding is more balanced than that. Based firmly in widely accepted historical accounts and quite recent developments in neurophysiology and more specifically NLP, this is neither the traditional 'no pain no gain' approach nor is it positive thinking short-term hype. Nor will it necessarily be easy, especially if you do not like the idea of change.

Everything I am recommending involves change — from fundamental lifestyle changes to a different attitude and even different beliefs where necessary. And change at a deep level is not easy for any of us. The good news is that there can be a lot of pleasure in the process once you make a start. And, even better, it doesn't take for ever. Some of the techniques, even for major belief change, can be carried out in less than half an hour. So, having removed, I hope, any mystique, it is more a matter of serious commitment than self-flagellation or self-suggestion.

As we have seen, just about everything we do and achieve is based on habits or unconscious competence. And however troublesome habits are, at least the negative kind, they can be changed by repetition and dogged commitment. And, in most cases, at least when we are carrying out the activity on a regular daily basis, this change can happen in about three weeks. This simple fact, and the fact that the sort of busy people reading this book cannot indulge in long self-development sabbaticals or personal coaching, provoked this three-week peak performance plan. Because it is a summary of the various actions suggested throughout the book, it also acts as a revision aid to enhance learning or a reference source you can use when faced with a specific performance challenge. I have assumed, ever the optimist, that you will have read the book before embarking on your three-week programme. This will increase the usefulness of the plan by about ten times.

In my book *NLP: The New Art and Science of Getting What You Want*, I added a 21-day programme — that is, giving daily activities. For the purpose of this plan I have just given flexible activity targets for each of the three weeks, so that a few misses now and again will not ruin your programme, and you can fit it in with existing commitments.

Refer back to the earlier chapters for the techniques you will need; they are mainly found in Chapters 7 and 8.

WEEK 1

1. Write down your goals. In what areas do you want to perform better and achieve more? Make them clear and specific.

2. Choose your top three and spend time visualising them as if they had happened. Don't imagine what you have to do to achieve them, but see, hear and feel what it will be like

when your outcome is fulfilled. This needs to be done in downtime (see Chapter 3) and you will have to give yourself at least twenty minutes for a mental rehearsal 'session'. Internalise each main goal in this way and do it as many times as you can fit in.

3. Recall and write down any eureka or flow experiences you have had. Note the circumstances and conditions that applied (Chapter 4). Check whether you can re-create these conditions.

4. Start to welcome pressure and expect good luck (Chapters 5 and 6).

5. Do the extended relaxation exercise in Chapter 7. If you have done this sort of exercise before or if you find it easy to wind down, one session may be enough. Otherwise repeat it three for four times throughout the week. Again you will need at least twenty minutes, and preferably longer, of uninterrupted time. Last thing at night is a good time, unless you find yourself falling asleep. Otherwise try first thing in the morning. Concentrate on visualising your inner special place (all in Chapter 7) in order to relax mentally as well as physically.

6. From Day 1 start to notice things and make a few of the lifestyle changes I suggest in Chapter 7 — starting gently, then building up. But make some change every day during your three-week period. Notice things all the time, wherever you are. This doesn't take up any time, you just need to be aware and will have to keep reminding yourself until it becomes a habit.

7. From the start, expect to receive insights about your goals, problems and anything on your mind. But don't worry if nothing happens. Whatever you do, don't try too hard to do anything. Start to trust your unconscious mind.

8. Use the change of state process (Chapter 7) to feel creative, calm, confident or whatever state of mind your particular

performance and goals demand. Set 'anchors' so that you can recall the state quickly when you need to.

WEEK 2

1. During this week try high speed relaxation (Chapter 7), at work or whenever you feel the need to be calm and in control. That is, when you are about to feel angry, annoyed, nervous, frustrated, upset, puzzled or panicky. Alternatively, find a short time to get away from your work and do a shortened relaxation session.

2. Start to reframe situations also, in each of the above circumstances in which you need to relax. Ask what other (than the obvious) meaning could there be for any behaviour, comments or event. See the big picture, the detailed picture, the best and worst scenarios, be objective (stand back) and subjective (put yourself into the situation), break a problem down, or 'chunk' it up (use the *sleight of mouth* technique in Chapter 8 as a reframing checklist). Whatever way you do it, always get new perspectives.

3. Make space for downtime (Chapter 3) every day.

4. Make lifestyle changes that give more time to yourself for freewheeling thinking. Don't feel guilty about daydreaming.

5. Mentally rehearse your top goals again. Develop a clear picture of what you want to do and be. Put yourself right in the picture — see things through your own eyes.

6. Identify three negative beliefs and apply the belief change process in Chapter 7.

7. Try instant state changes at work or wherever you are. Use the anchors you have already set.

WEEK 3

1. Keep up noticing, reframing and frequent downtime relaxing every day, and more frequently during the day.

2. Try one of the reframing techniques in Chapter 8 each day of this third week. You can apply more than one technique to the same goal or problem. Practise putting things right out of your mind when you have exhausted your thinking and cannot see a solution.

3. Try the Disney technique (Chapter 7) on a particularly difficult problem you want to be creative about.

4. Expect insights and also periods of flow and make a note of ideas as they come to you.

5. Keep making daily changes in your routines, one at a time.

6. Before the end of your third week make a commitment to take up new hobbies or interests and take a 'committing action' — make the first telephone call, tell somebody what you have decided, spend some money.

7. Make a commitment to continue each peak performance activity until you develop creative, high performance habits of unconscious competence.

FROM WEEK 4 ...

DAILY: Reframe, notice, create frequent downtime, change routines.

WEEKLY: Review and mentally rehearse goals. Apply a reframing technique to a specific goal or problem. Note any insights received and what you are doing about them.

Further Reading

Bandler, Richard & Grinder, John. *Frogs into Princes*. London: Eden Grove Editions. 1990.

Bandler, Richard & Grinder, John. *The Structure of Magic*. USA: Science and Behaviour Books. 1989.

Csikzentmihalyi, Mihaly. *Flow: The Psychology of Happiness*. London: Rider. 1992.

De Bono, Edward. *Water Logic*. London: Viking. 1994.

Dilts, Robert. *Strategies of Genius, Volumes I, II, & III*. USA: Meta Publications. 1994, 1995.

Gardner, Howard. *Creating Minds*. London: HarperCollins. 1994.

Higgins, James M & Majeed, Abdul S. *101 Creative Problem Solving Techniques*. USA: New Management Publishing. 1994.

Logsdon, Tom. *Breaking Through*. London: Addison-Wesley. 1993.

Robbins, Anthony. *Unlimited Power*. London: Simon & Schuster. 1989.

Index